# Valmiki Ramayana at a Glance
## (Untold Facts)

By

## Suripeddi Koundinya

M.Tech. Biotechnology
M.A. Astrology
M.A. Psychology

The Ramayana is a monumental work of literature, and its influence on Indian culture and religion is profound. The exact number of slokas (verses) varies slightly depending on the specific version, but it's generally around **24,000 slokas**.

There are many versions in the name of *Ramayana*: Valmiki *Ramayana*, Tulasi *Ramayana*, Kamba *Ramayana*, Bhaskara *Ramayana*, Molla *Ramayana* etc.
 But, all other *Ramayanas* follow Valmiki *Ramayana*. The essence of all versions is the same.

I have taken only the Valmiki *Ramayana* for facts.

The Valmiki Ramayana is a Hindu epic that tells the story of Prince Rama, his wife Sita, and his brother Lakshmana. The story begins with Rama's exile to the forest for fourteen years, followed by the abduction of Sita by the demon king Ravana. Rama, with the help of the monkey king Sugriva and his army, sets out to rescue Sita and defeat Ravana. After a fierce battle, Rama kills Ravana and rescues Sita. They return to Ayodhya, where Rama is crowned king.

The Valmiki Ramayana is a vast epic poem. Here's a breakdown of its structure:

3

- **Kandas (Books):** It consists of seven main books:
  1. **Bala Kanda:** Childhood of Rama.
  2. **Ayodhya Kanda:** Exile of Rama.
  3. **Aranya Kanda:** Life in the forest.
  4. **Kishkindha Kanda:** Meeting Sugriva and Hanuman.
  5. **Sundara Kanda:** Hanuman's journey to Lanka.
  6. **Yuddha Kanda:** The war between Rama and Ravana.
  7. **Uttara Kanda:** Events after the war.

First Published: April 2025

Second Print: June 2025

Third Edition: January 2026

## About the Author

**Suripeddi Koundinya** is a multidisciplinary author, educator, and researcher based in Hyderabad, India. With over 25 published works spanning psychology, astrology, biotechnology, statistics, and Indian mythology, he brings a unique blend of analytical depth and cultural insight to his writing.

His literary contributions include *Psychology Codex*, *Astrology Guide for Everyone*, *Stellar Inheritance*, and *Ocean of Rebirth*. In this volume, *Valmiki Ramayana at a Glance*, he explores 131 untold facts from the epic, offering readers a fresh and structured perspective rooted in both tradition and inquiry.

Koundinya holds advanced degrees in M.Tech Biotechnology, M.A. Psychology, and M.A. Astrology, and is a Life Member of the Indian School Psychology Association. His work reflects a commitment to ethical storytelling, spiritual clarity, and educational accessibility.

Acknowledgments

This book is lovingly dedicated to my family, whose support and blessings have shaped every word I write.

To my **father RadhaKrishna Murthy** and **mother Padmaja**, for instilling in me the values of discipline, devotion, and curiosity.

To my **wife Aparna**, whose quiet strength and unwavering encouragement has been my anchor through every creative endeavour.

To my **daughter Meenakshi**, whose innocence and joy remind me of the timeless stories we pass on.

To my **brother Koushik**, and his wife **Madhuri**, for their constant support and warmth—and to their daughter **Kshitija**, whose smile brings light to our lives.

This book is a tribute not only to the wisdom of Valmiki, but to the love and legacy of family.

# Table of Contents

# BALA KANDA

## (The Rama's Learning Age)

1) **Lord Rama**, at the tender age of **fourteen years**, embarked on a pivotal journey that would foreshadow his divine destiny. Accompanied by his devoted younger brother, **Lakshmana**, he joined the venerable **Sage Vishwamitra**. Their sacred mission led them deep into the **Dandakaranya forest**, a land plagued by malevolent **Rakshasas** who relentlessly sought to disrupt the solemn and sacred sacrificial rites of the ascetics.

During this arduous journey, Sage Vishwamitra, recognizing Rama's inherent purity and potential, imparted to him alone the potent secret knowledge of the **Bala and Atibala spells**. These mystical incantations, granted exclusively to Rama, were not merely words, but powerful tools that would grant him immense strength, unparalleled stamina, and freedom from hunger and thirst, preparing him for the monumental challenges ahead.

*(Bala kanda, sarga 22, Slokas 11, 12 & 14)*

2) Following Monkey kings and other animal born out of Gods to assist Rama in search for his consort Sita whom was abducted by demon king Ravala:-

a) Vali born from Indra (King of Devas)

b) Sugriva from Surya (Sun god)

c) Hanuman from Vayu (Wind god)

d) Jambavan from Lord Brahma

e) Taruna from Brihaspati (Jupiter)

3) Tataka (cursed Yaksha female demon) was the first killed by Rama at Vamana hermitage where 7 days of sacrificial rites are performing by sages in the forest of Tatakavanam. Sri Rama stopped the stones that Tataka rained on him with his arrows, and chopped off her arms. Lakshmana chopped off her ears and the tip of her nose. Sri Rama then aimed an arrow towards her chest, which made her fall down and die.

On the 5th day, sons of Tataka – Maricha and Subahu was killed. (*Bala kanda, sarga 26*)

4) As young **Rama** and **Lakshmana** journeyed alongside **Sage Vishwamitra**, the venerable ascetic, keen to impart knowledge of the world and its ancient histories, began to unfold the intricate tapestry of the kingdom of **Mithila**. His narratives were not merely stories, but windows into the profound events and divine interplays that shaped the very land they were traversing.

Among these enlightening tales, Vishwamitra recounted the poignant saga of **King Kusanabha** (a significant ancestor of Sita). It was told that Kusanabha's beautiful daughters, while sporting in the forest, incurred the wrath of **Vayudeva**, the powerful God of Wind. Their refusal to marry him, despite his advances, led to a severe curse: their bodies were grotesquely deformed, causing them to bear **hunchbacks**. To alleviate his daughters' suffering and miraculously make their humps disappear, King Kusanabha arranged for their marriage to the sage **Brahmadutta**. This unique sage himself bore an extraordinary origin, being born out of the sacred union between the revered **Sage Chuli** and the celestial **Gandharva woman Somada**.

Continuing the lineage, Vishwamitra further revealed that after these events, King Kusanabha diligently performed a significant sacrificial ritual, desiring a virtuous son. Through this rite, he was blessed with a son named **Gadhi**. This King Gadhi, in turn, became the direct father of none other than **Sage Vishwamitra** himself, thus connecting the narrator directly to the very history he was recounting. Vishwamitra also spoke of his own elder sister, **Satyavati**, a figure of great purity, who was wedded to the ascetic **Sage Ruchika**. This intricate web of divine births, curses, and alliances highlights the deep spiritual and historical connections that underpin the fabric of the Ramayana.

5) Story of **Skandha** who is known as **Lord Karthikeya**, narrated by sage Vishwamitra to Rama:-

"There was a mountain named Himavanta. His wife was Manorama. She was the daughter of the mountain Meru. They had two daughters called Ganga and Parvati (Uma). Parvati did fierce meditation to marry Rudra (Lord Shiva). All gods were afraid that Parvati might conceive a powerful Rakshasa. All of them went to Rudra and said, "If you release your semen the worlds cannot withstand that vigour. So contain it within you."

Rudra consented to that and left his semen on the earth. Gods fearing that the earth would split as soon as the semen of Rudra fell on it, prayed to the Lord of Fire (Agni). Agni burnt up that semen. It turned into a white mountain. Then a forest sprang on it. From it was born Shanmukha with six heads. Parvati got angry at the action of the gods and cursed them. "You have obstructed the birth of the child from my womb. You have separated my relation with Rudra. So your wives will also not conceive."

Gods approached Himavanta and prayed to him, "Ganga must not flow as she likes. She should flow in three ways." Himavanta was pleased and gave Ganga to gods. Ganga went to the abode of gods.

Once upon a time gods went to Brahma and said, "Our commander is doing penance. So appoint a new one." Brahma said, "Parvati cursed the gods to be childless, didn't she? So the god of fire will beget a son not by his wife, but by Ganga." The gods felt happy and prayed to Agni to beget a child. Agni went to the Ganges River and said, "Oh! Lady! You have to conceive through me. The gods pray so." Then the Ganges came to him in the form of a woman.

She conceived. Feeling distress, she said, "Agni! I am unable to bear this pregnancy, heavy with your vigour." Agni said, "Take this foetus and keep it on a mountain. Ganga, took out the foetus from the current of the river, placed it on the mountain which became white, when Agni had burnt the semen of Rudra earlier.

Some drops from that pregnancy had spilt on the earth and metals like gold, silver, copper and zinc had come into existence as a consequence.

A child was born out of that pregnancy. That child had six faces. Gods gave the child to the Krittika stars for rearing. The breasts of the stars sprouted milk. The child sucked the milk with six faces and became Kartikeya. The child drank for a day, grew up and defeated the armies of Rakshasas. The gods felt happy and made him their commander. Kartikeya is Kumara Swamy, he is Skandha.

6)  Sage Vishwamitra continues telling stories to Rama. He said that Ganga was descendant on earth escaping matt lock of Lord Shiva's hair because of severe penance of thousands of years by Sage Bhagiratha, who is Son of Dilip, grandson of Amsumanta, great grandson of Asamanjasa whose father was King Sagara.

On falling down on the earth, the Ganga split into seven branches and one branch followed Bhagiratha in the tracks of his chariot in its turns and twists. On the way, at a place, Sage Jahnu was performing a sacrifice. Ganga entered the hermitage threateningly. The sage got angry and swallowed Ganga completely. All the gods prayed to the sage Jahnu to release the Ganga. The sage was pleased and let the Ganga out through his ears. So the Ganga became sage Jahnu's daughter, Jahnavi. Later on, the Ganga went along with Bhagiratha to the netherworld and wetted the heaps of the ashes of Sagara's sixty thousand sons whom got cursed by sage Kapila.

# AYODHYA KANDA

## (Political Conspiracy behind Rama's Exile)

7) Among the many fascinating and lesser-known details embedded within the Valmiki Ramayana is the remarkable gift bestowed upon **King Kekaya**, the sovereign ruler of the prosperous Kekaya kingdom and father to the formidable Queen Kaikeyi, one of King Dasharatha's principal wives. King Kekaya possessed an extraordinary boon: the rare and mystical ability to **understand the languages of all living beings**, from the grandest beasts to the smallest insects. This unique power granted him an unparalleled insight into the hidden world of nature and its myriad inhabitants.

It was this very boon that led to an intriguing, albeit private, incident. One day, while resting, King Kekaya inadvertently overheard a conversation. Beneath the very cot where he lay, an ant, identified as **'Jrumbha'**, was engaged in a discussion. The content of this tiny creature's discourse, understood perfectly by the king, was evidently so amusing or surprising that he erupted into an uncontrollable fit of **loud laughter**. This seemingly innocuous act, the laughter of a king at the words of an ant, speaks volumes about the depth of his unique understanding and the unexpected humor or revelation that could emerge from the most humble of sources.

Such incidents underscore the intricate tapestry of life and communication that existed in the ancient world, often unseen and unheard by ordinary mortals.

8) In the intricate tapestry of the Valmiki Ramayana, few characters embody malevolence and manipulation as profoundly as **Manthara**. Far from a mere background figure, Valmiki's poignant description paints her as a truly wicked woman, whose physical deformity – a striking **hunchback** – was often seen as a reflection of her twisted inner nature. Her presence in the royal palace of Ayodhya was insidious, as she served as the primary catalyst, skillfully instigating the darkest and most destructive thoughts within Queen Kaikeyi.

What often remains an "untold" or overlooked detail is Manthara's intimate connection to Kaikeyi. She was not a mere palace attendant but a **'jnyaati daasi'** - a specific term used by the poet, signifying that she had arrived in Ayodhya as a servant directly from Kaikeyi's parental home. This distinction is crucial; it implies a deeper, almost familial bond and a long-standing loyalty, making her eventual betrayal and instigation even more potent and tragic. Her very duty was to safeguard and ensure **Kaikeyi's welfare**, yet she subverted this trust with cunning words and insidious counsel, planting seeds of doubt and ambition that would ultimately lead to Rama's exile and a cascade of sorrow.

*(Ayodhya kanda, sargas 7 to 9)*

9) The departure of **Lord Rama** for his fourteen-year exile in the dense Dandakaranya forest plunged Ayodhya into an unimaginable abyss of grief. Upon **Sumantra's** desolate return with the empty chariot, bearing the crushing news of Rama's irrevocable departure, **King Dasharatha's** anguish transcended mere paternal sorrow. Overcome by an unbearable pain that seemed to tear at the very fabric of his being, the King, in a moment of profound despair and revelation, confided in **Queen Kausalya** the hidden truth behind his torment: the dreadful **curse** that had shadowed his life for decades, now come to its bitter fruition.

This "untold fact" from Dasharatha's past illuminates the karmic threads that wove through his destiny. Long before his marriage to Kausalya and the birth of his illustrious sons, the youthful King, then a skilled archer, was engaged in a solitary hunt in a tranquil forest. His keen ear, mistaking the sound of a water pot filling for the rustling of a deer, led him to unleash an unerring arrow. Tragically, the arrow struck **Karana**, the innocent son of an ascetic, who was merely **collecting water from a river** at that fateful moment.

The grief-stricken father of the fallen boy, a venerable **Sudra sage**, whose eyes were now blinded by sorrow, discovered his dying son. In his profound bewailing, he uttered a chilling curse that echoed through the forest and into Dasharatha's soul: "Your Excellency! Just as I now suffer the unbearable pangs of separation from my beloved son, **you too shall ultimately die of the very same agony – the pangs of separation from your own son.**" This ancient malediction, a cosmic debt, now manifested with brutal precision, explaining Dasharatha's inconsolable despair as Rama, his most cherished son, left for the wilderness.

*(Ayodhya kanda, sarga 63, slokas from 14 to the last and also sarga 64, slokas from 1 to 58)*

10) King Dasaratha (King of Ayodhya) had 350 wives in addition to the three wives - Kausalya, Sumitra and Kaika. Queen Kausalya age was 6 when she got married to King.

*(Ayodhya kanda, sarga 39, sloka 36)*

11)   Amidst the swirling currents of fate and the impending sorrow of exile, the Valmiki Ramayana occasionally offers glimpses into the profound spiritual

wisdom that guided **Lord Rama**. While much of the epic focuses on heroic deeds, righteous conduct, and dramatic events, there are moments of deep philosophical insight that often remain "untold facts" for the casual reader. One such revelation comes directly from Rama himself, a statement of profound spiritual truth: **'God does not appear to the eye.'**

This isn't a declaration of atheism or divine absence, but rather a fundamental tenet concerning the nature of Ultimate Reality. Spoken at a moment of significant emotional and existential reflection, Rama's words illuminate the understanding that the Supreme Being, the divine essence, is not perceivable through ordinary, physical senses. The divine transcends the limitations of material perception. It suggests that true communion with God, or the realization of the divine, requires an inner vision, a purified mind, and a consciousness that extends beyond the superficial.

This subtle yet powerful statement from Rama underscores the spiritual depth of the Ramayana. It reminds us that while divine forms may appear in earthly narratives, the true nature of God is formless, limitless, and accessible only through inner awakening and profound spiritual insight. It posits that faith and devotion are not about witnessing a physical manifestation, but about recognizing the omnipresent, unmanifest truth that permeates existence, a truth that resides beyond the grasp of the mere eye.

*(Ayodhya kanda, sarga 30, sloka 33)*

12) Among the many cherished episodes of the Ramayana, the crossing of the Ganges River by **Lord Rama**, **Sita**, and **Lakshmana** during their exile is a moment of profound significance, often romanticized in popular retellings. Commonly, narratives depict **Guha**, the revered King of the Nishada (Boya) tribe and a staunch devotee of Rama, personally taking up the oars to ferry them across the sacred river. However, for those delving into the meticulous details of **Valmiki's original Ramayana**, an intriguing "untold fact" emerges, offering a more nuanced understanding of this pivotal moment.

The authentic accounts reveal that while Guha's devotion was indeed boundless and his presence at the Ganges crucial, he did **not** himself act as the oarsman for the divine trio. Instead, demonstrating his profound respect, strategic leadership, and the immense hospitality of his tribe, **Guha had only sent his most skilled and trusted men** to manage the boat and ensure the safe passage of Rama, Sita, and Lakshmana across the vast waters. His role was that of a benevolent king and a loyal friend, overseeing the arrangements and providing all necessary provisions for their journey, rather than performing the physical act of rowing.

13) As the moment of exile loomed, the selfless love and foresight of Ayodhya's royal family ensured that **Sita** was provided with an array of necessities befitting her stature, even in adversity. The Valmiki Ramayana meticulously records **King Dasharatha's** poignant gestures: gifts of exquisite saris, precious ornaments, and essential cosmetics **for** Sita, meant to sustain her

grace even in the wilderness. For **Rama and Lakshmana**, provisions of a different kind were prepared: robust shields, potent weapons, utilitarian baskets, a sturdy crow-bar, and various other implements crucial for survival in the dense forest. This thoughtful provisioning, demonstrating immense care, is a known and touching detail.

What often goes "untold," however, is a subtle yet significant logistical gap in the narrative. Sage Valmiki, with his characteristic precision, details the initial stages of this journey. He vividly describes the careful arrangement of these articles within the royal chariot before their departure from Ayodhya. Furthermore, he explicitly narrates the meticulous process of shifting these very provisions into the boat when the divine trio prepared to cross the sacred River Ganga, guided by Guha's men.

Yet, a curious silence follows this precise detailing. Once across the mighty Ganga and deep within the wilderness, **there is a striking absence of any mention in the story regarding how all these numerous and often weighty articles actually reached the deeper parts of the Dandakaranya forest**. The venerable poet, in his masterful storytelling, seems to have **cleverly left this practical point without explicit mention**.

This subtle omission naturally provokes a compelling question for any discerning reader: Who, then, bore the considerable responsibility of transporting these essential items, day after day, through the challenging terrain of the forest?

Given his unwavering devotion, immense strength, and self-appointed role as protector and provider for Rama and Sita during their exile, it is incredibly natural to conclude that **Lakshmana, the tireless and ever-vigilant younger brother, must have shouldered this unseen**

**burden.** His unwavering commitment likely extended beyond mere protection to the physical carrying of their very sustenance and tools, a silent testament to his profound service.

14) Far from a strictly vegetarian diet, the epic clearly states that **Rama and Lakshmana, true to their Kshatriya dharma and the necessities of forest life, engaged in hunting for their sustenance.** Valmiki precisely narrates instances where, for the sake of food, they skillfully brought down various animals. Specifically, they killed a **boar, a powerful bison, a swift deer, and a distinctive spotted deer.** This act of hunting was not for sport but for survival, providing essential nourishment in an environment devoid of cultivated fields or readily available vegetarian provisions.

Thus, the poignant reality is that **the ascetic life of Rama, the very embodiment of righteousness, indeed began with meat-eating.**

*(Ayodhya kanda, sarga 52, sloka 102)*

15) **Lord Rama**, the epitome of composure, forbearance, and unwavering righteousness, is rarely depicted as expressing harsh judgment or resorting to sharp words, especially towards his elders. Yet, in a powerful and often "untold" moment within the **Valmiki Ramayana**, even

Rama, in the throes of the profound injustice inflicted upon him, employs a strikingly potent term to describe his step-mother, **Kaikeyi**. He uses the word 'arrogance', but the original Sanskrit expression chosen by the poet, **'sowbhagya madamohita'**, conveys a far deeper and more nuanced condemnation.

*(Ayodhya kanda, sarga 53, Sloka 15)*

16) At a crucial juncture in their journey, **Sita**, the embodiment of purity and devotion, addressed a towering Banyan tree with immense reverence, calling it **'Oh great tree, Shyama!'** The epithet 'Shyama' (dark-hued or dusky) likely referred to its ancient, sprawling form and dense foliage, indicating its immense age and spiritual significance. With folded hands and a sincere heart, she earnestly prayed to this venerable arboreal giant, imploring its mercy and seeking its blessing for a safe and comfortable completion of their arduous exile.

This act of prayer by Sita, the wife of Sri Ramachandra, to a tree, as well as her subsequent acts of reverence towards stones, rivers, and similar natural elements frequently observed throughout the epic, was not merely an isolated gesture. Instead, it serves as a powerful illustration of a widespread and deeply ingrained spiritual practice among human beings in Ancient Bharatavarsha. Our ancestors, recognizing the sheer power, vastness, and life-sustaining qualities of nature, used to worship the **oldest trees, towering hills, life-giving rivers, boundless oceans, and indeed, each and every phenomenon that was huge in magnitude or awe-inspiring in Nature**. They profoundly believed that these grand manifestations of the cosmos possessed a living spirit or divine energy and held the power to influence their destinies and fulfill their desires. This reverence, exemplified by Sita's simple yet profound prayer, underscores the pantheistic and deeply ecological consciousness that permeated ancient Indian society, where the divine was perceived not just in temples, but in every majestic aspect of the natural world.

*(Ayodhya kanda, sarga 55, sloka 25)*

17) Following the devastating demise of his beloved father, **King Dasharatha**, and the meticulous completion of the necessary funeral rites, **Bharata** found himself at a profound crossroads. Despite being presented with the throne of Ayodhya, his unwavering commitment to righteousness and his deep fraternal love compelled him to vehemently refuse the crown. Instead, his heart was set on a singular, arduous mission: to seek out his elder brother, **Lord Rama**, who, along with his devoted wife **Sita** and loyal brother **Lakshmana**, had already begun their ascetic life at the serene **Chitrakuta Mountain**.

Bharata's departure from Ayodhya was not a solitary undertaking. He embarked upon this noble quest in his chariot, accompanied by a vast entourage of elders, including revered ministers, learned priests, and the grieving royal mothers. This grand procession underscored the collective sorrow of Ayodhya and the fervent hope that Rama would return to assume his rightful place. An often "untold fact" of this journey highlights the crucial role of strategic intelligence: Bharata received vital information about Rama's precise whereabouts at Chitrakuta Mountain directly from the **spies dispatched by Guha**, the loyal King of the Nishadas, whose deep knowledge of the forest and his unwavering allegiance to Rama proved invaluable.

Guided by this intelligence, Bharata's formidable procession journeyed through the challenging terrains. Their path led them to the sacred **Ganges River**, where, once again, the unwavering devotion of Guha came to the fore. Guha's boats were promptly provided, ensuring the smooth and respectful crossing of Bharata and his entire retinue. After traversing the mighty river, their journey culminated in their arrival at the tranquil hermitage of the revered **Sage Bharadwaja**.

*(Ayodhya kanda, sarga 91)*

18) Even amidst the serene beauty and spiritual tranquility of the **Chitrakuta Mountain**, the heart of **Lord Rama** remained inextricably linked to his beloved Ayodhya. While he stoically embraced the ascetic life of exile, his inner world was a rich tapestry of memory and profound acceptance. In a moment that offers a tender and often "untold" glimpse into his royal and compassionate psyche, Rama articulated a series of striking comparisons, transforming his immediate surroundings into echoes of the home he had left behind.

As meticulously recorded in *Ayodhya Kanda, Sarga 95, Sloka 15*, Rama himself revealed this unique perspective. He poignantly **compared the majestic Chitrakuta itself with Ayodhya**, seeking solace in its natural grandeur as a substitute for his lost capital. The pristine and gurgling **River Mandakini**, flowing gracefully through the region, was likened to the sacred **Sarayu**, the lifeblood of his ancestral city, thereby imbuing his exile with a sense of continuity and spiritual connection.

However, the most profound and perhaps most revealing comparison was his contemplation of the **wild animals** that roamed freely through the Dandakaranya forest. In a testament to his expansive compassion and his longing for his subjects, Rama perceived these innocent forest dwellers as akin to the very **people of Ayodhya**. This wasn't merely a fanciful thought; it was a deep acknowledgment of their constant presence, their uncorrupted nature, and perhaps the simple, unvarnished life they led, mirroring the pure affection he held for his citizens. Through these comparisons, Rama found a way to bridge the chasm of separation, transforming his challenging circumstances into a reflective sanctuary where the essence of his former life could still be cherished. This revelation showcases not only his acceptance of destiny but also his inherent divinity and benevolence, extending his kingly concern to all beings, even in the depths of his personal sorrow.

19) The highly anticipated arrival of **Bharata** at Chitrakuta Mountain, accompanied by a vast retinue from Ayodhya, was a moment charged with emotional complexity. While Bharata's earnest purpose was to convince Rama to return and claim the throne, **Lord Rama**, with his profound insight and perhaps even a divine intuition, perceived subtle yet ominous cues that foreshadowed a great tragedy. This particular moment offers an "untold fact" into Rama's acute awareness and his deep, unspoken anxieties.

As Bharata's grand procession approached, Rama keenly observed the details. He noticed a distinct absence of the usual auspicious signs and customary royal fanfare traditionally associated with King Dasharatha's well-being and the thriving state of his kingdom. Valmiki, in his masterful narration, highlights this acute perception. The lack of specific regal banners, the subdued demeanor of the accompanying ministers, or perhaps the absence of particular imperial symbols that would denote the reigning monarch's good health – these were the subtle, yet weighty, indicators that troubled Rama's mind.

It was this striking deficit in the expected protocol and auspicious display that led Rama to a chilling and grievous **premonition**. Long before any direct communication of the news, Rama's sharp intellect and loving heart connected these missing 'signs' with a grave possibility. He harbored a profound doubt, asking himself, and perhaps Lakshmana, the unspoken question: **whether King Dasharatha was still alive or not.**

*(Ayodhya kanda, sarga 97, sloka 16)*

20) Rama himself is telling Bharata. "Your mother has not unjustly done this. Our father promised your grandfather that he would give kingdom to you only", Rama himself acknowledged the fact. Then why did Rama prepare for coronation in spite of knowing this fact? Moreover, why does he abuse Kaika? Are there qualities of a good man in Rama's words or actions? He revealed the secret now because it won't create any problem  and Bharata has said he would give kingdom to Rama! The entire Valmiki *Ramayana* is based on this single sloka.

*(Ayodhya kanda, sarga 107, sloka 3)*

21) Kausalya is making Sumitra feel happy that Lakshmana will also enjoy royal pleasures after Rama becomes king. "Don't worry that your son is doing drudgery", says Kausalya.    *(Ayodhya kanda, sarga 103, sloka 7)*

22) The emotionally charged encounter at Chitrakuta saw **Bharata** making a fervent, almost desperate, appeal to **Lord Rama** to abandon his exile and return to assume the throne of Kosala. In his unyielding determination to convince Rama of his royal duty, Bharata employed every conceivable argument, pushing the boundaries of conventional discourse. Among these powerful pleas, there emerges a truly striking and often "untold fact": Bharata, usually depicted as the epitome of righteousness and adherence to tradition, surprisingly articulated arguments that bordered on **'atheism'**, or at least a deeply pragmatic skepticism.

In a poignant moment of his persuasive rhetoric, Bharata explicitly challenged the perceived benefits of a purely ascetic life, directly questioning the spiritual efficacy of solitary meditation. He uttered the startling query: **'Who knows what benefit or no benefit accrues from meditation?'**

Bharata's argument was fundamentally utilitarian. He was not genuinely an atheist but was appealing to Rama's sense of immediate, tangible responsibility as a Kshatriya king, prioritizing the welfare of the people and the stability of the kingdom over personal spiritual pursuits that, in his view, offered an uncertain "benefit." He subtly suggested that the direct, observable benefits of good governance far outweighed the unquantifiable spiritual gains of meditation in a forest. This audacious line of questioning, coming from such a devout character, underscores the extreme pressure Bharata felt and the lengths to which he would go to fulfill what he perceived as the higher dharma – ensuring Rama's rightful place on the throne and the prosperity of Ayodhya. It's a testament to the complexity of Valmiki's characters, who grapple with nuanced ethical dilemmas even while embodying ideals.

*(Ayodhya kanda, sarga 106, sloka 20)*

23) 'Kings who rule the world become rulers merely because they speak the truth', thus spoke Rama! It follows that the rich are the ones who speak the truth. The poor tell lies and hence in such a sorry plight! It also means, the reason for the existence of Masters and Servants is also the speaking of truth and untruth! *(Ayodhya kanda, sarga 109, sloka 16)*

24) Bharata, filled with sorrow and regret, condemns his mother Kaikeyi's actions and refuses to accept the throne gained through injustice. He declares his unwillingness to rule Ayodhya in Rama's absence, considering it a great sin and disgrace. His devotion to dharma and his elder brother is evident as he insists on bringing Rama back. He continues to express his grief, emphasizing that Ayodhya belongs to Rama and not to him. When he finally meets Rama, he earnestly pleads with him to return, presenting moral and logical arguments. However, Rama, bound by his father Dasharatha's promise, remains resolute in fulfilling his exile. This emotional episode highlights the unwavering righteousness of both brothers—Rama's commitment to duty and Bharata's selfless love, making it one of the most profound moments in the Ramayana.

*(Ayodhya kanda, sarga 109, sloka 34)*

25) All the sages in Chitrakuta mountain area are very particular that Rama must kill Ravana. Plans with regard to killing Ravana had been going on much before and even without reference to the incident of Surpanakha.

*(Ayodhya kanda, sarga 112, sloka 4)*

*26)* The emotional crescendo at Chitrakuta Mountain reached its peak when **Bharata**, having desperately implored **Lord Rama** to return to Ayodhya and reclaim his rightful throne, finally accepted Rama's unyielding commitment to his fourteen-year exile. Faced with Bharata's unwavering devotion and his refusal to rule in Rama's absence without a legitimate symbol of authority, Rama conceived of a solution that was as ingenious as it was deeply symbolic – a moment often recounted but whose profound layers of meaning serve as a crucial "untold fact" of leadership and dharma.

In an act that transcended conventional royal protocol, **Rama, without any opposition or hesitation**, acquiesced to Bharata's plea for a tangible representation of his kingship. Rama meticulously placed **his own sandals upon the throne**. This simple act, however, was imbued with immense spiritual and political weight. More strikingly, before placing them, Rama deliberately **put his feet into the sandals and then removed them**. This seemingly small gesture was not merely a ceremonial formality; it was a powerful act of investing his divine authority, his very presence, and his sacred resolve into the sandals themselves.

These actions transformed the humble sandals into powerful regalia, becoming the de facto symbol of Ayodhya's sovereignty during Rama's absence. This unprecedented delegation allowed **Bharata** to govern the kingdom not as its king, but as a devoted regent, ensuring that he upheld his vow of loyalty and did not usurp his elder brother. The sandals represented Rama's constant, albeit unseen, guidance and legitimate rule, ensuring that dharma continued to be maintained in Ayodhya. This unique solution highlights Rama's unparalleled wisdom, his ability to navigate complex ethical dilemmas, and his profound understanding of duty and delegation even when physically absent. It remains a powerful testament to the enduring power of symbolic leadership and selfless devotion in the Valmiki Ramayana.

*(Ayodhya kanda, sarga 112, sloka 22)*

27) Amidst the trials of their forest exile, Rama, Sita, and Lakshmana sought refuge in various hermitages, offering protection to the ascetics from the demonic forces. However, an often "untold" and deeply revealing episode from the **Valmiki Ramayana** exposes a moment of profound doubt, even among the most revered sages, regarding Rama's immediate capacity for protection. This incident, detailed in **Ayodhya Kanda, Sarga 116 (all slokas)**, presents a stark contrast to the common perception of Rama's unshakeable divine power.

The events unfolded with palpable tension. The resident sages, displaying **ominous signs** and gestures of unease, began to express their growing fear. Initially, a subtle disquiet pervaded the hermitage, perhaps leading Rama to inwardly assess the situation and consider the potential vulnerabilities, particularly concerning Sita and Lakshmana. This burgeoning anxiety culminated when an **old sage reported the imminent arrival of Khara**, a formidable Rakshasa known for his cruelty, escalating the sages' fears into open alarm.

The turning point came with the sages' direct accusations, revealing their deep-seated trepidation. In **Slokas 10 and 13**, they articulated their grievances to Rama with chilling clarity: **'The Rakshasas are harassing us because of you. Their harassment has increased after your arrival here!'** This was a direct and painful indictment, implying that Rama's presence, rather than providing immediate safety, had inadvertently drawn greater demonic aggression upon their peaceful sanctuary.

Their concerns escalated into a pragmatic demand for Rama's departure. In **Sloka 22**, the sages delivered a blunt assessment of his protective capabilities: **'You are with your wife. However valorous you may be, it will be difficult for you to protect your wife. You also leave this hermitage!'** This statement is particularly striking, as it casts doubt on Rama's prowess, suggesting that even his inherent valor might be insufficient to safeguard Sita amidst the rising demonic threat, compelling him to abandon their refuge.

Most poignantly, **Sloka 23** confirms the profound impact of their words: '**Rama, with counter-arguments, could not stop the sages who were talking so and leaving!**' This is the ultimate "untold fact" – despite Rama's logical counter-arguments and assurances, he failed to assuage their fears or convince them of his protective might. The sages, prioritizing their own safety, chose to evacuate their hermitage, demonstrating their pragmatic lack of faith in Rama's immediate ability to shield them from the intensified Rakshasa attacks. This episode vividly illustrates the harsh realities of exile, where even divine figures faced human doubts and pragmatic challenges, adding a layer of compelling realism to the epic narrative.

28) Having departed from the sacred Chitrakuta Mountain, a place now laden with the bittersweet memories of Bharata's visit and the unsettling departure of the local sages, **Lord Rama**, **Sita**, and **Lakshmana** continued their arduous journey deeper into the Dandakaranya forest. Moving with a disciplined grace, often depicted with Rama leading, followed closely by the delicate Sita, and the ever-vigilant Lakshmana bringing up the rear, they sought out the guidance and blessings of venerable ascetics. Their path ultimately led them to the serene and hallowed hermitage of the illustrious **Great Sage Atri**, a paragon of virtue, who resided there with his beloved and profoundly chaste wife, **Anasuya**.

The arrival at Atri's ashram marks a significant juncture, not least because it introduces the extraordinary figure of Anasuya. While her name is well-known, the depth of her spiritual power and compassion often remains an "untold fact" in popular retellings. Anasuya was no ordinary ascetic; her unwavering devotion and unparalleled spiritual austerities had endowed her with incredible Siddhis (supernatural powers). It is recounted that her penance, stretched over an astonishing **ten thousand years**, was so potent that it profoundly impacted the very fabric of nature.

During a period of severe and widespread drought, when life itself withered, it was Anasuya's immense spiritual energy that miraculously **produced luscious fruits on barren trees and caused water to flow abundantly in the parched Ganges River**. This divine intervention was a testament to her profound tapasya and her boundless empathy for all living beings. Her ability to command the elements underscores the immense spiritual might possessed by the ancient sages and their wives, whose self-discipline and piety could literally alter the natural world.

*(Ayodhya kanda, sarga 117, slokas from 5 to 13)*

# ARANYA KANDA

## (Mysteries of the Forest and Golden Deer Deception)

29) In Dandakaranya forest, Rama and Lakshmana came across demon Viradha (Son of Jaya & Satahrada). Viradha was once a gandharva name Tumbura. He received curse from Kubera to become brahma-rakshasa. Now he tried to abduct Sita. His shoulders were cut-off by both Rama and Lakshmana.

*(Aranya kanda, sarga 3, slokas 14 to 24)*

30) The Dandakaranya forest, a realm both beautiful and perilous, was home to many austere sages who sought spiritual liberation amidst its solitude. During their arduous exile, **Lord Rama**, **Sita**, and **Lakshmana** encountered numerous such revered figures. One particularly striking and often "untold" incident involves the venerable **Sage Sarabhanga**, whose life culminated in an act of extraordinary spiritual will and devotion.

Upon meeting Rama, the aged Sage Sarabhanga revealed that he had long awaited Rama's arrival, holding onto his mortal coil solely for this divine darshan. Having achieved the highest fruits of his immense penance, he now sought to shed his physical body and ascend directly to the supreme abode. In a demonstration of ultimate detachment and yogic power, Sarabhanga prepared for his final departure.

In a scene of profound spiritual significance, the sage, with a resolute mind, caused a **blazing fire pit** to appear before him. Then, in a truly astonishing act, and **in the solemn presence of Lord Rama, Lakshmana, Sita, and other gathered sages, Sage Sarabhanga calmly and deliberately threw himself into the consuming flames.** This was not an act of despair or self-destruction, but a controlled and conscious yogic departure, a final offering of his physical form.

The purpose of this extraordinary self-immolation was clear and direct: to **depart to heaven, specifically Vaikuntha Dhama**, the eternal abode of Lord Vishnu. This event stands as a powerful testament to the efficacy of intense asceticism (tapasya) in ancient Hindu belief, where a perfected yogi could consciously shed their body to attain direct liberation and union with the divine. Sarabhanga's fiery ascent underscores the profound spiritual power attainable through sustained penance and highlights the belief that the mere presence of a divine being like Rama could facilitate such an ultimate liberation, ensuring a direct path to the highest spiritual realms.

31) As **Lord Rama**, **Sita**, and **Lakshmana** continued their arduous journey through the mystical depths of the Dandakaranya forest, they encountered places of profound natural beauty intertwined with ancient legends. One such remarkable spot was the enchanting **Lake Panchapsara**, a shimmering body of water whose very existence held a captivating "untold fact" – a testament to the immense power of asceticism and the subtle machinations of the divine.

This pristine lake was not a natural formation but a wondrous creation of the revered **Sage Maandakarni**. This ancient sage had embarked on an extraordinary and prolonged period of severe penance, standing immersed in water for countless years. His rigorous spiritual austerities generated immense power, causing concern even in Svarga (heaven). Fearing that Maandakarni's accumulating spiritual strength might eventually challenge his own celestial dominion, **Lord Indra**, the king of the gods, resorted to his characteristic strategy to disrupt such potent tapasya. He dispatched **five celestial damsels, or Apsaras**, renowned for their unparalleled beauty and seductive charm, to tempt and distract the sage.

However, in a twist that highlights Maandakarni's supreme spiritual mastery – an "untold fact" that defies common notions of ascetics succumbing to temptation – the sage did not fall from his penance in the conventional sense. Instead, utilizing his extraordinary yogic power, Maandakarni **created the magnificent Lake Panchapsara specifically for these five divine damsels**. He transformed the very instruments of his potential downfall into a beautiful abode for them, integrating them into his spiritual realm, or perhaps, showcasing his complete mastery over desire by providing them a place without breaking his vows. This unique act allowed the Apsaras to reside there, enjoying its pristine waters, while Maandakarni continued his spiritual practices, now seemingly undisturbed by their presence.

Thus, Lake Panchapsara stands as a silent monument to the unassailable power of a perfected ascetic, a place where divine temptation was met not with surrender, but with a display of transformative spiritual might. Its story, encountered by the royal exiles, adds another layer to the complex spiritual landscape of the Ramayana.

32) As **Lord Rama**, accompanied by Lakshmana and Sita, ventured deeper into the sacred and often perilous Dandakaranya forest, he frequently shared profound insights and ancient narratives with his devoted brother. These stories, far from being mere diversions, served to educate Lakshmana about the spiritual significance of the very lands they traversed and the extraordinary beings that graced them. Among these crucial lessons, Rama eloquently narrated the awe-inspiring deeds of the venerable **Sage Agastya**, a colossal figure whose spiritual prowess profoundly shaped the southern regions.

One of the most striking and often "untold facts" about Agastya is his decisive intervention against the malevolent **Rakshasa brothers, Ilvala and Vatapi**, who terrorized Brahmins and ascetics. These demonic siblings employed a gruesome and cunning trick: Ilvala, disguised as a benevolent Brahmin, would invite unsuspecting travelers for a feast. His brother, Vatapi, would then transform into a ram, which would be slaughtered and served as a meal. After the Brahmins had consumed the meat, Ilvala would call out, "Vatapi, come forth!" whereupon Vatapi would violently burst out of the victims' stomachs, killing them instantly. Agastya, however, with his divine insight, saw through their vile deception. When invited, he consumed the disguised Vatapi, and upon Ilvala's customary call, simply declared, "Vatapi has been digested!" With his immense yogic power, he permanently absorbed and destroyed Vatapi within his body, liberating countless Brahmins from their torment and putting an end to the Rakshasas' heinous acts.

Beyond this heroic feat, Rama also recounted Agastya's pivotal role in **ceasing the formidable growth of the Vindhya Mountain**. This mountain range, in its unchecked arrogance, had begun to swell skywards, growing so tall that it eventually obstructed the path of the very Sun and Moon, plunging vast regions of the Earth into perpetual shadow and disrupting the cosmic order. The gods, troubled by this celestial obstruction, sought Agastya's intervention. As the great sage journeyed south, he approached the towering Vindhya. Out of profound reverence for Agastya's spiritual might, the mountain humbly bowed down to allow him passage. Agastya, seizing this opportune moment, commanded the Vindhya to remain bowed until his return from the south – a return he famously never made. In this ingenious manner, Agastya, through his sheer authority and the mountain's respect, permanently quelled its arrogant growth, restoring the balance of the cosmos and the natural order of day and night.

These two extraordinary tales, narrated by Rama, highlight Agastya's unparalleled spiritual power, his unwavering commitment to protecting dharma, and his profound influence over both demonic forces and natural phenomena. They stand as testaments to the incredible feats performed by enlightened sages in the Ramayana's ancient world.

33) After enduring a significant portion of their exile—a arduous **ten years** spent traversing forests and encountering various ascetics—**Lord Rama**, along with his steadfast wife **Sita** and devoted brother **Lakshmana**, sought a more settled and strategic dwelling for the remainder of their forest sojourn. It is a compelling, yet often "untold," detail from the Valmiki Ramayana that Rama initially expressed a desire to spend these remaining years in the immediate vicinity of the revered **Sage Agastya's hermitage**, perhaps seeking continuous spiritual guidance and the profound security offered by the sage's immense power.

However, the sagacious **Agastya**, with his unparalleled foresight and understanding of the unfolding cosmic design, offered a different counsel. Despite the honor and safety Rama's presence would have brought to his own ashram, Agastya wisely suggested that they establish their new residence at **Panchavati**.

(Aranya kanda, sarga 11, sloka 88)

34) The serene yet perilous expanse of the Dandakaranya forest witnessed a pivotal encounter when **Surpanakha**, the formidable sister of the Rakshasa king Ravana, first approached **Lord Rama**. Drawn by his unparalleled beauty, she made overt advances, seeking to win his affection. In response, Rama, ever the upholder of dharma and possessing a keen understanding of the subtle nuances of communication, did not directly reject her with harshness. Instead, in a moment that reveals his

protective instincts and strategic mind, he chose to paint a stark picture of the **dangers inherent in their ascetic life**, a facet of their exile that often remains an "untold fact" in popular retellings.

During his conversation with Surpanakha, Rama deliberately detailed the grim realities of living in the wild. He emphasized that the forest was a realm of constant threat, where not only ferocious **animals** roamed, but also powerful and malevolent **Rakshasas** lay in wait. To underscore his point, Rama subtly referenced past terrifying encounters, thereby validating his warning with grim experience. He likely alluded to, or had fresh in his mind, experiences with formidable beings such as:

- **Kakasura**, a Rakshasa who had attacked Sita in the form of a crow, a vivid and deeply personal memory for Rama, showcasing the insidious nature of the threats they faced and the divine intervention required to save Sita.
- **Viradha**, a monstrous Rakshasa who had violently abducted Sita and Lakshmana before being vanquished by Rama, serving as concrete proof of the immediate and tangible dangers that lurked in the wilderness.

Crucially, Rama pointed out how these dangers specifically posed a threat to **Sita**, highlighting her vulnerability and the immense responsibility he bore for her safety. His words were a double-edged sword: a factual enumeration of the perils and a subtle discouragement to Surpanakha, hinting that life with him was far from the romantic ideal she envisioned. This conversation reveals Rama's foresight and his protective nature, emphasizing that his exile was not merely a spiritual retreat but a constant battle for survival against an ever-present, malevolent force, making the very presence of Sita a heightened responsibility amidst such grave peril.

35) The forest of Dandakaranya, a realm of both spiritual austerity and lurking peril, became the stage for a pivotal encounter that ignited the flames of the Great War. When **Surpanakha**, the audacious Rakshasa sister of King Ravana, encountered **Lord Rama**, she was instantly enamored by his divine beauty. Despite his polite refusals and his unwavering commitment to his wife Sita, Surpanakha's desire escalated into a relentless and aggressive pursuit, a situation that tested Rama's famed composure.

In a move that highlights his adherence to dharma and his attempt to dissuade her without outright violence, **Rama initially directed Surpanakha to Lakshmana,** playfully suggesting that he, being unattached, might be a suitable match. Lakshmana, mirroring his brother's resolve to uphold their ascetic vows, also firmly declined her proposal, even mocking her with pointed words about her unsuitability. The repeated rejections, coupled with Lakshmana's biting sarcasm, fueled Surpanakha's wounded pride into a furious rage.

It is at this critical juncture that a vital, yet often "untold," fact emerges: feeling utterly humiliated and insulted, Surpanakha, in a fit of uncontrollable fury, directly attacked Sita. Her intent was clear – to harm, perhaps even devour, Rama's beautiful wife, whom she perceived as the ultimate impediment to her desires. This direct threat to Sita, a defenseless lady, served as the immediate and undeniable catalyst for Lakshmana's swift and decisive action.

Without waiting for an explicit command from Rama, Lakshmana, driven by his fierce devotion and his solemn vow to protect Sita at all costs, acted on his own initiative. With blinding speed, he drew his sword and, in a brutal act of defense, **cut off Surpanakha's nose and ears**. This horrific disfigurement was not an act of wanton cruelty, but a necessary and immediate response to an imminent danger to Sita's life.

*(Aranya kanda, sarga 18, slokas 20, 21)*

36) Surpanakha, with streams of blood on her entire body, went to Khara, who was in the nearby locality.

Khara is the son of Surpanakha's mother's younger sister. In the past, Ravana had conquered many territories and kept Khara, with some army, as his royal representative at a place called *Janasthan* in *Dandakaranya*. Ravana, in a war he had waged in the past, had intentionally killed Vidyujihwa, husband of Surpanakha.

Later, when Surpanakha was grieving, Ravana had consoled her that he would take care of her without any dearth for anything and had asked her to live in Janasthan. Since then Surpanakha had been living in Janasthan. Khara had been looking after her with affection. Surpanakha was destroyed by both Ravana and Rama. Ravana had killed her husband; Rama had had her ears and nose severed.

*(Aranya kanda, sarga 19, slokas 14 to 16; sarga 34, sloka 11)*

37) Lord Rama single-handedly with Sword and Vaishnava Bow (thousands of Arrows at a time) killed more than 14,000 soldiers of King Khara of Janasthan, his chief commander Dushana and his general Trisira (Son of Ravana) in Dandakaranya forest to protect Sita and Lakshmana who hide in cave.

A spy called Akampana went to Ravana and informed him about the battle in Janasthan.

*(Aranya kanda, sarga 30, shlokas 30, 31)*

38) Sita sees the golden Deer (Maricha in disguise) and insists that Rama capture it for her. She expresses an intense desire for its hide, stating that she wants to play with it and take it to Ayodhya.

54

Normally, Sita is not materialistic, but this time she is deeply fascinated by the deer. This suggests that the Maya (illusion) of Ravana's plan was working on her.

This request leads to Rama leaving the ashram, Lakshmana following later, and Ravana abducting Sita, setting the stage for the Great War.

(Aranya Kanda, Sarga 43, Slokas 18-19)


39) On hearing the distressful words of Rama (Maricha Voice) shouting "Save Me Sita! Lakshmana... Sita asked Lakshmana to go and protect Rama. Sita harshly accuses Lakshmana of conspiring with Bharata to let Rama die, questioning his loyalty. Despite serving her for years and fulfilling her requests, Lakshmana refuses to leave the ashram, as he is duty-bound to protect her. If Lakshmana had gone instead of Rama, Ravana's plan would have failed, as Rama would have easily defeated him, altering the course of the epic.

(Aranya kanda, sarga 45, slokas 24, 25)

40) Sita became more furious of Lakshmana's prayer of consoling her that nothing happened to Lord Rama,. - "You can never beguile me with these deceitful words. Never did you have any reverence for your brother. When danger befalls my husband I shall end my life jumping into the Godavari River. I shall sacrifice my life by consuming poison or hanging myself or jumping into the fire or jumping from the top of a mountain but never

shall I touch another man even with my foot" so saying she *covered the hem of the upper garment around her shoulders.* (Aranya kanda, sarga 45, slokas 36, 37)

41) The tranquil hermitage at Panchavati, meant to be a sanctuary for **Sita** during Rama's and Lakshmana's pursuit of the illusory golden deer, became the scene of the Ramayana's most devastating event: Sita's abduction. The Valmiki Ramayana, with its meticulous details, reveals a chilling "untold fact" about how **Ravana**, the mighty ten-headed king of Lanka, executed this nefarious act,

relying not on brute force initially, but on insidious cunning.

Driven by an insatiable lust and a thirst for revenge after his sister Surpanakha's disfigurement, Ravana employed a masterstroke of deception. He transformed his formidable Rakshasa form and appeared before Sita in the benign and venerable **attire of a mendicant sage (a *sanyasi* or *bhikshu*)**. This disguise was crucial: clad in ochre robes, with matted hair, carrying a staff, and holding a begging bowl, he perfectly mimicked the appearance of a holy man, thereby disarming Sita's natural caution.

As he approached the isolated hermitage, Ravana, the epitome of malevolence, began to speak. Instead of a simple request for alms, he launched into a torrent of eloquent and detailed **praise for Sita's unparalleled beauty, describing her captivating features meticulously from top to toe.** This was not merely a polite compliment; it was a calculated act of psychological manipulation, designed to flatter and distract the lonely Sita, making her feel safe and perhaps even admired by a seemingly harmless holy man. Every word was chosen to lull her into a false sense of security, to break down her reserves, and to draw her out of the protective line (Lakshmana Rekha) that Lakshmana had drawn.

(Aranya kanda, sarga 46, slokas 17 to 22)

42) While in Pushpak Viman Chariot of Ravana carrying her on his lap, Sita cried all along for help – 'birds, trees, mountains, etc.., to inform Lord Rama of her abduction.

Finally, Jatayu (bird of 60,000 years old then) come to rescue Sita by flying to Vimana fought with beak and toe nails. It scratched Ravana's back with its beak. Ravana placed Sita down and began fighting with Jatayu with his legs and hands. He cut off Jatayu's wings and feet with a sword. Jatayu fell to the ground. The anklet bells on Sita's left foot broke off and fell down jingling. Still,

58

some more ornaments fell down like stars falling from the sky.

*(Aranya kanda, sarga 49, slokas 27, 28, 34, 35)*

43) Sri Rama killed Maricha, and killed another animal, took its flesh and went away quickly towards Janasthana. "On hearing Maricha's cries, the foxes are howling weird. The birds are crying frightfully." Rama was afraid that some danger might befall Sita.

*(Aranya kanda, sarga 44, sloka 27)*

44) "I will go to the cottage only if Sita is alive. Otherwise
I will give up my life at this tree (which he lean upon)", says Rama. He was not allowing Lakshmana to speak and he doesn't know what has happened to Sita. He just imagining drowned in the ocean of sorrow.

*(Aranya kanda, sarga 58, sloka 9)*

45) Lord Rama deeply immersed himself unable to bear the separation of his beloved Sita and think of 10 different ways of conditions - Desire (*Abhilasha*), Mental union (*Manassangamam*), Resolve (*Sankalpam*), Description of qualities (*Guna varnana*), hatred (*Pradveshamu*), the fire of Sex (*taapam*), Sacrifice of Self-interest (*Abhimata tyagam*), Madness (*Unmaadam*), Fainting and Death.

*(Aranya kanda, sarga 60, last slokas)*

46) Unknown to the situation that Ravana abducted and taken Sita to Southwards Lanka, Sri Rama and Lakshmana started searching for Sita in Northwards direction walking 6 miles from Janasthana crossing Dandakaranya and entered Krowncharanya forest.

47) They (Rama and Lakshamana) came across a huge Rakshasa Kabandha (son of Dhanu) in the forest who was cursed by sage Sthuula Sirassu and about to eat them. Both brothers chopped his hands when Rakshasa was holding them to eat. Later on his request, Lakshmana cremated him. Rising from the ashes, Kabandha who no longer a Rakshas but a Gandharva begin to tell to take help of Sugriva (Son of Vanara Riksharajas) whom reside in Rishyamukha Mountain near the bank of Pampa Lake.
 Kabandha also tells "There are six ways of tackling things in this world: *Sandhi, Vigraham, Yanam, Asanam, Dwaidibhavam and Samaasryam.*

*(Aranya kanda, sarga 72, sloka 21)*

48) As **Lord Rama** and **Lakshmana** continued their sorrowful search for Sita, their journey through the desolate yet spiritually charged forest brought them to the pristine vicinity of Pampa Lake. It was here, near its northern bank, that they came upon the humble cottage of **Sabari**, an aged and devout female ascetic. Sabari was

no ordinary hermit; she was a fervent devotee who had been patiently awaiting the arrival of Rama for countless years, sustained by the prophecy of her guru, Sage Matanga, that she would one day have the sacred *darshan* of the Lord himself.

Upon their arrival at her simple dwelling, which was located within or very near the hallowed grounds of **Sage Matanga's hermitage** (where she was the sole surviving disciple), Sabari's joy knew no bounds. She welcomed the princes with heartfelt reverence, offering them humble hospitality. For years, she had meticulously collected the sweetest fruits of the forest, awaiting this very moment. Having had the profound blessing of **Lord Rama's divine *darshan***, the culmination of her life-long penance and unwavering devotion, Sabari understood that her earthly purpose was fulfilled.

This deeply touching moment, marked by the pure exchange of devotion and grace, rapidly transitioned to Sabari's final, transformative act—an "untold fact" that powerfully demonstrates the concept of liberation through devotion. Having achieved the ultimate spiritual goal, the old **Sabari, in a deliberate and conscious act of yogic departure, threw herself into a blazing fire pit**. This was not an act of despair, but a sacred sacrifice of her mortal coils, a final offering of her physical form. Through this fiery ascent, she transcended the earthly realm, attaining immediate liberation and joining her revered gurus and the divine in Vaikuntha Dhama.

(Aranya kanda, sarga 75, sloka 3)

49) As **Lord Rama** and **Lakshmana** continued their agonizing search for Sita, their journey led them to the mesmerizing region surrounding **Pampa Lake**. In this poignant phase of the epic, the celebrated poet **Valmiki** pause the narrative of sorrow and pursuit to offer an exceptionally vivid and detailed description of this natural wonder.

Valmiki's narrative transcends mere geographical description, painting a rich tapestry of flora that made Pampa Lake a sanctuary of unparalleled beauty. He speaks of countless **intertwining creepers**, their tendrils weaving together like living garlands: the fragrant **Jaji**, the delicate **Punnaga**, the vibrant **Vasanthi**, the exquisite **Nagamallika**, the unique **Nilakosa**, the lush **Purnika**, the elegant **Sirisha**, and the striking **Karavira**. These intertwining beauties adorned the shores, creating a vibrant, verdant embrace around the shimmering waters.

The lake itself was a spectacle of aquatic splendor, its surface dotted with an array of **blossomed, fragrant flowers**. Valmiki specifically mentions the passionate hues of **red lotuses**, the pristine purity of **white lotuses**, and the enigmatic depths of **black lilies** (or night-blooming lotuses), each contributing to a breath-taking aquatic mosaic that delighted the senses.

The surrounding arboreal landscape was equally magnificent, boasting a diverse and luxuriant collection of trees: the fruit-bearing **Neredu** and **Moradi trees**, the sturdy **Panasa trees (jackfruit)**, the vividly flowering **Karnikari trees**, the imposing **Tommiravi trees**, the ubiquitous **Mango trees**, the sacred **Tilakas**, the deep blue **Nili Ashokas**, the charming **Kadambas**, the aromatic **Rakta Chandanas (red sandalwood)**, and the graceful **Spandanas**. This rich variety of trees, with their varied foliage, flowers, and fruits, contributed to the overall enchanting atmosphere of the lake.

Valmiki's comprehensive and poetic portrayal of Pampa Lake, far from being a mere filler, serves as a poignant contrast to Rama's internal anguish. It highlights the inherent, captivating beauty of ancient India's natural world, a source of temporary solace even amidst profound grief, and stands as a testament to the Ramayana's timeless celebration of nature's majesty.

# KISHKINDHA KANDA

## (Hidden Secret of Monkey King)

50) After the devastating abduction of Sita, **Lord Rama** and **Lakshmana** began their search, which led them to the region around Pampa Lake and eventually to the famed **Rishyamukha Mountain**. This particular mountain held a unique sanctity, being the only place where Sugriva, the exiled Vanara king, felt safe from the wrath of his elder brother, Vali. It is at this critical juncture that a poignant and often "untold fact" about the initial encounter between the divine princes and the Vanara chief unfolds, revealing a profound sense of fear and misunderstanding.

As Rama and Lakshmana approached Rishyamukha, their appearance, armed with **swords, bows, and arrows**, and their resolute gait, struck terror into the heart of **Sugriva**. He was not alone in his apprehension; he was hiding behind a large rock, accompanied by his trusted confidantes: his father-in-law **Tarudu**, the skilled engineers **Nala** and **Nila**, and the exceptionally wise **Hanuman**. Despite the princes' divine aura, Sugriva, constantly living under the immense shadow of Vali's persecution, could only interpret their formidable presence through the lens of his deep-seated paranoia.

His immediate and overwhelming assumption was that **his elder brother, Vali, had dispatched these powerful, armed strangers to finally kill him.**

This profound fear highlights the extent of Vali's tyranny and the desperate, vulnerable state in which Sugriva lived. He saw not potential allies, but assassins. This misjudgement, born of chronic fear, underscores the gravity of his predicament and why he, despite being a king, was reduced to a fugitive. It also serves as the precise reason for Hanuman's subsequent diplomatic mission, where he was tasked with cautiously approaching the newcomers to ascertain their true intentions, thereby bridging the chasm of fear with wisdom and trust.

*(Kishkindha kanda, sarga 2, sloka 10)*

51) Following **Sugriva's** initial terror upon spotting the armed princes, **Lord Hanuman**, renowned for his wisdom and discretion, was dispatched to ascertain their true identities and intentions. This crucial first encounter, a masterclass in diplomacy and observation, offers a compelling "untold fact" about Hanuman's approach: he didn't reveal his true form or purpose immediately. Instead, he presented himself in the humble **attire of an ascetic**, a mendicant Brahmin, standing reverently before **Rama and Lakshmana**.

His approach was marked by a stream of profound praise, designed to gauge their character and intentions while subtly revealing his own discerning intellect. Hanuman began by acknowledging their paradoxical appearance, stating, **"You look like sages, but you must be kings or emperors!"** This astute observation immediately recognized their spiritual aura juxtaposed with their regal bearing and weaponry. He then proceeded to describe the captivating effect of their divine presence on the very landscape: **"These mountains and hills were glittering in the reflection of your complexion on them!**

**Water in the Pampa appears as if it is mixed with gold!"** (Kishkindha Kanda, Sarga 2, Slokas 24 & 25). This vivid imagery conveyed not just flattery, but a genuine perception of their radiant, almost luminous, essence.

Hanuman continued to shower them with discerning praise, eloquently describing the inherent brightness and divine glow emanating from their bodies, their noble faces, and even their formidable bows and swords. This elaborate eulogy served a dual purpose: to disarm any suspicion the princes might have, and to gather information about their reactions. Only after this astute and respectful overture, having observed their demeanor and received a response from Rama, did Hanuman finally **reveal his true identity, stating his belonging to the Vanara (monkey) race** and his position as a **minister under the valorous King Sugriva**.

*(Kishkindha kanda, sarga 2, slokas 24 & 25; sarga 3, slokas 20 to 23)*

52) Taking residence in Malaya Mountain Cave, Sugriva did not in fact have any idea of making friends with Rama. He had instructed Hanuman to enquire about them and had not told him to bring them to him.

On learning that Rama and Lakshmana were not Vali's followers, Hanuman had got the idea of getting Vali killed by Rama. Hanuman was very much pleased on hearing the words Lakshmana, making up his mind, to get victory over Vali, intended to make Sugriva befriend Rama and Lakshmana. (*Kishkindha kanda, sarga 3, last sloka*)

53) Rama told Sugriva: "I'll kill Vali who abducted your wife. I shall see you get back your wife."

In same manner, Sugriva assured Rama saying - "I shall get back your wife. You will cast off the agony of separation from your wife. Even if she is in the nether world or in the skies, I shall get back your wife."

(Kishkindha kanda, sarga 5, sloka 27)

54) The nascent alliance between **Lord Rama** and **Sugriva** at Kishkindha was born out of mutual need: Rama sought help in locating Sita, and Sugriva desperately needed liberation from his tyrannical brother, Vali. Despite Rama's initial assurances, Sugriva, having suffered years of bitter exile and humiliation under Vali's oppressive rule, was still plagued by a deep-seated apprehension. His prolonged suffering had cultivated an understandable scepticism, making him doubt if any power could truly overcome Vali, let alone a stranger. This underlying, yet unvoiced, doubt in Sugriva's mind forms a crucial "untold fact" that highlights Rama's profound empathy and his absolute commitment to his word.

Rama, with his inherent understanding of human nature and his keen perception of Sugriva's emotional state, recognized this silent hesitation. He knew that for their alliance to be truly robust and effective, Sugriva needed more than just a promise; he needed an unbreakable assurance, an unshakable faith in Rama's resolve. It is precisely for this reason that Rama, in a moment of extraordinary solemnity and earnestness, made a declaration that resonated with the very core of his being.

As recorded in **Kishkindha Kanda, Sarga 7, Sloka 22**, Rama looked directly at Sugriva and declared with absolute conviction: **"I have never uttered a lie. Nor will I utter [a lie] in future. I swear to you on truth."** This was no ordinary vow. For Lord Rama, **Truth (Satya)** was not merely a virtue; it was his very essence, the foundational pillar of his Dharma. This explicit, powerful oath underscored his unwavering adherence to veracity, serving as the ultimate guarantee of his word.

The sheer earnestness, with which Rama articulated this oath, emphasizing his lifelong commitment to truth, was designed to completely dispel Sugriva's lingering doubts. It signified Rama's profound eagerness to forge an unbreakable bond of trust, demonstrating that his promise to kill Vali was not a fleeting assurance but an immutable decree. This "untold fact" showcases Rama's strategic understanding of alliance-building, his compassionate recognition of Sugriva's trauma, and his unwavering integrity, cementing the foundation for the monumental events that would follow.

*(Kishkindha kanda, sarga 7, sloka 22)*

55) Following the formation of their pivotal alliance, **Lord Rama** sought to understand the deep-seated animosity that existed between **Sugriva** and his formidable elder brother, **Vali**. It was then that Sugriva, seeking to justify his plight and secure Rama's unwavering support, recounted the tragic genesis of their bitter enmity in the Vanara kingdom of Kishkindha. This narrative, a crucial "untold fact" in understanding Sugriva's exile and Vali's subsequent fate, reveals a complex web of misunderstanding and unfortunate circumstance.

Sugriva explained that the devastating rift began with the arrival of a powerful **Rakshasa named Mayavi**. Mayavi, the son of Maya and brother of the monstrous Dundubhi, challenged Vali to a ferocious combat, seeking to avenge his deceased brother. Vali, never one to back down from a fight, swiftly pursued Mayavi into a dark and cavernous **cave**. Before entering, Vali instructed Sugriva to guard the cave entrance and, if he did not return after a certain period, to assume his demise.

Days turned into weeks, and from within the cave, Sugriva eventually heard the terrifying sounds of a prolonged struggle, followed by a sudden, eerie silence, and then streams of blood flowing out. **Assuming his brother Vali had tragically met his end** in the battle with Mayavi, and acting upon the desperate pleas of the distraught ministers and citizens who feared for Kishkindha's leadership, **Sugriva ascended the throne.** He then sealed the cave entrance with a massive rock, believing he was protecting the kingdom from Mayavi's potential emergence and honoring Vali's presumed sacrifice.

However, unknown to Sugriva, Vali had indeed vanquished Mayavi after a prolonged struggle and had then managed to break free from the sealed cave. Upon his return to Kishkindha, Vali was enraged to find Sugriva ruling as king. Misinterpreting Sugriva's actions as a deliberate act of betrayal and a greedy usurpation of the throne, **Vali violently kicked his brother out of the Kingdom.** He confiscated Sugriva's wife, Ruma, and relentlessly pursued him, forcing Sugriva to live a life of constant fear and hiding in the Rishyamukha Mountain, which Vali could not enter due to a sage's curse.

This tragic tale of misunderstanding and Vali's subsequent wrath, eloquently narrated by Sugriva, solidified Rama's understanding of the injustice meted out to his new ally. It laid the groundwork for Rama's intervention and his solemn vow to help Sugriva reclaim his rightful place.

*(Kishkindha kanda, sarga 9, sloka 18)*

56) The initial confrontation between **Vali** and **Sugriva**, orchestrated by **Lord Rama** as the first step towards restoring Sugriva's throne, culminated in a devastating defeat for the younger Vanara prince. Sugriva, severely beaten and psychologically scarred by his powerful brother, returned to Rama not with meekness, but with an outburst of profound despair and raw fury. This dramatic moment, often an "untold fact" in its full emotional intensity, reveals the very human aspects of Sugriva's character and the complexities of the divine alliance.

Consumed by humiliation and a deep sense of betrayal, Sugriva launched into a bitter tirade against Rama. His words, sharp and accusatory, laid bare his wounded pride and lingering fear. He openly questioned Rama's intentions and perceived inaction, exclaiming: **"You showed me your valour, asked me to challenge Vali to battle and now made the enemy beat me. Having done all this, now what do you think about? Had you told me then itself that you would not kill Vali, I would not have gone to fight with him."** (Kishkindha Kanda, Sarga 12, Slokas 25 & 28). This emotionally charged accusation was a testament to Sugriva's desperate state, making him feel utterly exposed and abandoned by the ally in whom he had placed all his trust. He perceived Rama's inaction as a direct betrayal, questioning his word and his integrity.

Rama, however, responded to Sugriva's emotional outburst not with anger, but with remarkable patience and candor. In a crucial revelation, an "untold fact" that addresses a common point of contention, Rama clarified his inability to strike Vali in the initial attempt. As stated in **Slokas 30 to 32** of the same Sarga, Rama explained: **"As both of you resembled with one another in ornaments, attire, body size, gait, voice, complexion, looks, valour and words, I was beguiled."**

This astonishing admission from Rama underscores the extraordinary and almost identical likeness between Vali and Sugriva. In the chaotic heat of battle, distinguishing between the two brothers—who were identical in every perceivable aspect, from their physical appearance and ornaments to their very voice and valor—was an impossibility. Had Rama shot his arrow, there was a grave risk of inadvertently striking Sugriva instead of Vali. This moment reveals a rare instance of Rama's pragmatic dilemma, where his divine prowess was momentarily confounded by the physical similarity of his targets. It highlights his meticulous precision, his aversion to collateral damage, and ultimately, his unwavering commitment to justice over hasty action, thereby reinforcing the profound trust between them.

*(Kishkindha kanda, sarga 12, slokas 25 & 28, 30 to 32)*

57) Vali says to his wife Tara, "Don't grieve that Rama will do anything to me. Because, will Rama commit the sin of killing an innocent one?. I shall not kill Sugriva in battle. I shall suppress his arrogance. I shall send him felicitating him with blows", Vali abided by the rules of a just fight. His view was that none will fight unjust battles.

*(Kishkindha kanda, sarga 16, slokas 5, 7 & 8)*

58) After Rama aimed at Vali shooting his bow pierced the chest of Vanara, later abuses him by saying "Till now, I was not aware that you call yourself a virtuous man but in reality you are an unjust man and a sinner. You are a man who commits base deeds. You don't show it but do harm. You are of a bad temper. You don't have any courtesy. You simply carry a bow. Being lustful, you behave as your senses *drag* you".

*(Kishkindha kanda, sarga 17, slokas 13 to 52)*

59) After the coronation of Sugriva and since he started living on Rishyamuka Mountain for 4 months, Rama has been doubt whether Sugriva would help him or not as agreed upon after Rainy season.

*(Kishkindha kanda, sarga 28, slokas 62 to 66)*

60) Sugriva along with Lakshmana from Kishkindha came to visit Rama at cave in a palanquin. Rama caught hold of him and began to preach sermons. See! "King of Vanara! A king ought to divide dharma (duty), artha (wealth), kama (sexual pleasure) depending on the appropriate time". The time has come to locate Sita (it has been 8 months since Sita got abducted) and wage a battle against Ravana. You have to discuss this matter with your ministers.

Sugriva's reply: "Owing to your grace, I have acquired the Vanara kingdom, which is permanent. Crores of

Vanaras - who will kill Ravana including his relatives and get Sita – are approaching you."

(*Kishkindha kanda, sarga 38, slokas 16 to 24 and also sarga 39, slokas up to 7*)

61) With **Vali's** demise and **Sugriva's** rightful ascension to the throne of Kishkindha, the focus of the epic swiftly shifted to the solemn promise made to **Lord Rama**: the relentless search for **Sita**. This pivotal moment saw the full might of the Vanara kingdom spring into action, a mobilization on an unparalleled scale, revealing a significant "untold fact" about the vast resources and unwavering loyalty at Rama's disposal.

Under the direct and urgent command of **King Sugriva**, **crores of Vanaras** (monkeys) began their fervent preparations for dispatch. This wasn't just a small detachment but an immense, unprecedented army, symbolizing the colossal collective effort required for their monumental task. Their mission was twofold and crystal clear: to diligently **search for Sita** across the vast and unknown lands, and crucially, to **locate the elusive kingdom of Lord Ravana**, the demon king who held her captive.

Among these countless warriors, specific **ministers and heroes** were singled out to lead these crucial expeditions, each a figure of immense strength, wisdom, or strategic importance. The Valmiki Ramayana meticulously lists these key commanders who stepped forward, ready to face any challenge:

- **Satavali**
- **Gavaksha**
- **Nila** (a chief architect and son of Agni, instrumental in building the bridge to Lanka)
- **Nala** (another chief architect and son of Vishwakarma, equally crucial for the bridge)
- **Darimukha**
- **Dadhimukha**
- **Durmukha**
- **Jambavan** (the wise and ancient bear-king, renowned for his strategic counsel and experience)
- **Gandhamadanu**
- **Rambhu**
- **Dhumru**
- **Vanasu**
- **Maindu**
- **Dwividhu**
- **Angada** (Vali's son and Sugriva's nephew, a valiant prince who would lead a key search party)
- **Indrajanuvu**
- **Vahni**
- **Sushena** (Tara's father and a renowned physician, highlighting the diverse skills within the Vanara forces)

- **Tarudu** (Ruma's father, a figure of familial importance within Sugriva's trusted circle)

*(Kishkindha kanda, sarga 40, slokas 10 to 15)*

62) Following the grand mobilization of Vanara forces, **King Sugriva** meticulously organized his search parties, assigning specific directions and leaders to each. The most crucial of these expeditions was dispatched towards the **South**, the presumed direction of **Ravana's** elusive kingdom and, by extension, **Sita's** captivity. This detailed briefing, an "untold fact" revealing Sugriva's profound geographical knowledge and strategic planning, underscores the epic scale of their undertaking.

Leading this vital southern contingent were some of the most formidable and sagacious Vanara chiefs: the valiant prince **Angada**, alongside the resourceful **Tarudu**, the mighty **Hanuman** (whose role in this mission would prove unparalleled), the insightful **Sushena**, the powerful **Nila**, and the wise elder **Jambavan**. Their journey commenced from Kishkindha itself, a realm now widely identified with the historic **Anegundi village in Koppal district, Karnataka State**.

What makes Sugriva's instructions truly remarkable is his encyclopaedic knowledge of the terrains they were to traverse. He did not merely point them southward; he provided an incredibly detailed itinerary, naming a vast array of **rivers, oceans, and mountains** that lay on their formidable path. His verbal map included:

- The familiar **Rishyamukha** Mountain, which they had just left.
- Distant ranges like **Udayagiri** and **Hemagiri**, suggesting lands rich in minerals or unique flora.
- The formidable peaks of **Pariyatra** and **Vajra**, indicating treacherous, unyielding territories.
- The vast **Viraha** and the renowned **Vindhya** mountains, signifying significant geographical divides.
- Mystical or potentially symbolic peaks like **Meru** and **Malaya**, guiding them through diverse landscapes.
- The monumental **Mahendra** Mountain, which would later become a critical landmark for Hanuman's leap across the ocean.
- Other ranges such as **Pushpitam**, **Kunjara**, **Bhogavati**, and **Rishabha**, each likely holding unique characteristics or spiritual significance known to the Vanara king.

*(Kishkindha kanda, sarga 42, slokas 12 & 13)*

63) Having dispatched the crucial southern contingent, **King Sugriva** then turned his attention to the western direction, entrusting its exploration to **Sushena**, the wise and venerable father of Queen Tara. This assignment, an "untold fact" in its specific and intriguing details, reveals the vast and often mystical geography of the ancient world as understood by the Vanaras, going far beyond mere physical landmarks to include places of profound divine significance.

Sugriva commanded Sushena to take a substantial force of **two lakh (200,000) Vanaras** and meticulously described the path they were to follow towards the west. His instructions were not just geographical but imbued with legendary details, highlighting unique and powerful locations:

- **Hemagiri and the Confluence of Sindhu:** Sugriva began by directing them towards a mountain called **Hemagiri**, a place perhaps known for its golden hues or rich resources. Here, he described a significant landmark: the confluence where the mighty **Sindhu River** (Indus River) merges with the sea, indicating a vast coastal region to explore.
- **The Enigma of Winged Lions:** More astonishingly, Sugriva spoke of a region inhabited by **lions with wings**. This fantastical detail hints at the extraordinary, almost mythical creatures believed

to exist in the farthest reaches of the world, emphasizing the unknown wonders and perils the Vanaras might encounter.

- **Chakravanta Hill and Divine Deeds**: The most sacred and intriguing detail was the mention of a hill called **Chakravanta**. Sugriva revealed its divine significance, stating that it was here that **Sri Mahavishnu**, in an act of immense valor, slew a Rakshasa named **Hayagriva**. From this victory, Vishnu acquired his divine discus, the **Chakra weapon**. Furthermore, on the same hill, Vishnu also vanquished another demon named **Panchajana** and acquired his iconic conch shell, the **Panchajanya**. This specific account embeds the Vanara's quest within a larger cosmic narrative, connecting their mission directly to the deeds of the supreme deity.

*(Kishkindha kanda, sarga 42, slokas 27 & 28)*

64) The search for Sita in the southern direction, led by **Angada**, **Hanuman**, **Nila**, and **Jambavan** along with countless other Vanaras, was nearing its appointed deadline. Weeks had turned into months, and despite their exhaustive efforts, the elusive location of Ravana's kingdom remained a mystery. It was amidst this growing despair and exhaustion that they stumbled upon a colossal and ancient **Cave called Ruksha**. Deep within its

mystical confines, they encountered **Swayamprabha**, the radiant daughter of Meru Savarni, who revealed she guarded the cave under the ancient command of the celestial nymph Hema.

While their encounter with Swayamprabha and the wonders of her hidden realm were extraordinary, it provided no answers regarding Sita's whereabouts. The crushing realization that they had failed to locate Sita, coupled with the imminent expiry of the deadline set by Sugriva, plunged the Vanara leaders into profound fear and hopelessness. Overwhelmed by the terrifying prospect of returning to Kishkindha empty-handed and facing Sugriva's wrath, **Angada proposed a desperate and defiant course of action: to remain within the cave and embrace a fated end, fearing the execution order from Sugriva more than death itself.**

It was **Hanuman** who stepped forward, attempting to console and encourage Angada to reconsider, urging a return to Kishkindha to face their king. However, Angada's despair had festered into bitter resentment, leading to a raw and cutting indictment of Sugriva's character – a truly powerful and often "untold fact" of internal strife within the Vanara leadership.

Angada's scathing reply to Hanuman's reprimand, detailed in **Kishkindha Kanda, Sarga 53, from Sloka 27,** was a torrent of accusations, revealing his deep-seated distrust and fear:

**"Sugriva does not have a stable mind, purity of soul, mercy, honesty, valour and serenity."** Angada launched, completely denouncing his uncle's moral and mental fortitude.

He then sharply brought up the controversial aspect of Sugriva's past: **"One who took his elder brother's wife, who was like his mother, as his wife, when his brother was still alive is condemned by the world."** This accusation directly attacked Sugriva's conduct regarding

Vali's wife, Ruma, highlighting a contentious point of contention and moral judgment.

Angada continued his condemnation, recalling the very incident that sparked their exile: **"How can a man be just who closed the entrance of the cave when his brother had entered the cave?"** He painted Sugriva as treacherous, recalling the crucial moment when Sugriva had sealed the cave, believing Vali dead, a decision that ultimately led to Vali's wrath and Sugriva's banishment.

Finally, Angada concluded his lamentation, driven by sheer terror of his uncle's perceived avarice: **"Sugriva - who did unpleasant things secretly, who was harsh and who was base - will imprison me and punish me, out of his avarice for the kingdom - thus he wailed."** His words revealed a deep fear of retribution, portraying Sugriva as a ruthless and greedy monarch.

*(Kishkindha kanda, sarga 53, from sloka 27)*

65) After weeks of relentless and ultimately fruitless searching, the Vanara heroes, led by **Angada**, **Hanuman**, **Jambavan**, and **Nila**, found themselves at the edge of the formidable **Mahendra Giri Hill**, gazing upon the boundless expanse of the southern ocean. Despair had gripped their hearts, for the deadline set by Sugriva had passed, and Sita remained unfound. It was in this moment of

profound despondency, as they contemplated their grim fate, that destiny intervened through an unexpected and extraordinary figure.

From his perch on the mountain, an ancient and massive vulture appeared: **Sampati**, the elder brother of the valiant Jatayu. A truly poignant "untold fact" of the epic is Sampati's tragic physical state: he was a bird **without wings**, having lost them long ago in a selfless act of protecting his younger brother from the scorching rays of the sun. His colossal, wingless form and immense age bore witness to millennia of existence. Hearing the Vanaras lamenting their plight and speaking of Ravana and Jatayu, Sampati stirred.

With a voice heavy with age and sorrow, Sampati revealed the crucial, life-changing intelligence the Vanaras so desperately needed. He directly informed **Jambavan, Angada, Hanuman, and the other gathered Vanaras** about the precise whereabouts of Sita, whom he had witnessed being abducted by the demon king: **Ravana, King of Lanka, had indeed carried Sita away to his island kingdom.**

More critically, Sampati provided the vital geographical detail that transformed their despair into renewed purpose: Lanka, Ravana's formidable fortress, was located a staggering **100 Yojanas** (approximately 800 miles) away from their current position on **Mahendra Giri Hill**, across the vast and treacherous ocean. Sampati, due to his immense age and his unique vantage point from the sky (before his wings burned), had witnessed Ravana forcibly carrying Sita across the ocean, granting him this unparalleled, eye-witness knowledge.

*(Kishkindha kanda, sarga 59, up to 5 slokas)*

# SUNDARA KANDA

## (Beauty of Lanka and Valour of Hanuman)

66) After the momentous leap from Mahendra Giri Hill, **Lord Hanuman** embarked on his epic aerial journey across the vast southern ocean towards Lanka. This incredible flight, a testament to his immense power and unwavering devotion, was far from unobstructed. The Valmiki Ramayana meticulously details a series of formidable challenges he encountered mid-air, each revealing a different facet of his extraordinary character - truly "untold facts" that define his unparalleled strength and cunning.

His first encounter was with **Mainaka Mountain**, a benevolent peak that rose from the depths of the ocean. Mainaka, grateful for the protection once offered by Vayu, Hanuman's divine father, during a celestial conflict, emerged from the waters to offer Hanuman a brief respite and a place to rest. Hanuman, however, respectfully declined, acknowledging the mountain's kindness with a gentle touch before continuing his urgent mission, unwilling to delay even for a moment.

Next, a more insidious challenge presented itself in the form of **Surasa**, the formidable mother of the Nagas. Sent by the gods to test Hanuman's intelligence and resourcefulness, Surasa assumed a gigantic, monstrous form and demanded that Hanuman enter her mouth, declaring it her destined prey. In a brilliant display of wit and mastery over his form, Hanuman initially expanded his body to an enormous size, forcing Surasa to open her mouth wider and wider in an attempt to swallow him. Then, with lightning speed, he suddenly **reduced his body to the size of a thumb**, darted into her cavernous mouth, and emerged instantly through her ear, tricking her and fulfilling her condition without being truly consumed.

The third and most dangerous obstacle was **Simhika**, a fearsome Rakshasa who possessed the unique power to capture the shadow of any passing creature and drag them into her gaping maw. As Hanuman flew overhead, Simhika ensnared his shadow, attempting to pull him down. Recognizing the unusual nature of her power, Hanuman reacted with decisive ferocity. He rapidly **expanded his body to a gargantuan size within her very mouth**, tearing her internal organs apart, and then burst forth, leaving the demoness vanquished.

Finally, after overcoming these perilous trials through a combination of strength, intelligence, and divine grace, Hanuman arrived at the periphery of Lanka. Strategic in his approach, he **reduced his body size** to an inconspicuous form to avoid immediate detection. He then **climbed down on Lamba Mountain**, a peripheral peak, from where he gazed upon his ultimate destination: the magnificent, heavily fortified **City of Lanka**, perched majestically on the towering peaks of **Trikuta Mountain**, glowing in the distance. This initial glimpse was the culmination of his arduous journey and the prelude to his solitary infiltration.

67) Hanuman thinks what will happen if he goes and tells Rama that Sita was nowhere to be seen. "If I tell him the unpleasant words, Rama will give up his life and will not live. Seeing Rama, Lakshmana will not live. Hearing about the death of Rama and Lakshmana, Bharata will not live.

Seeing Bharata's death, Satrughna will not live. This is how the chapter on deaths in Ayodhya went on for some time.

Later in Kishkindha, "Seeing the plight of Rama, Sugriva who is a truthful man, will give up his life. Ruma gives up her life because of her husband's death. Stricken with grief Tara will give up her life. Then how can Angada stay alive? Stricken with grief over the death of their king, all the Vanaras will jump enmasse from the peaks of the mountain and give up their lives. They will break their heads with palms and fists. They will give up their lives by consuming poison, by hanging themselves, by entering the fire, by fasting and by falling on the swords." Ayodhya and Kishkindha will perish if Rama dies.

*(Sundara kanda, sarga 31, slokas 13 to 38)*

68) On seeing Sita in Asokavanam, Hanuman thought, "Sita is a heap of beauty. A great devoted wife. She is waiting for a sight of her husband. Just as a boat sinks in the sea due to the weight of the goods, Sita is drowned in the sea of sorrow due to the separation from her husband.

Rama knows pretty well how to rule a kingdom, how to pacify elephants and horses but it seems he does not know how to love his wife! If ruling the three worlds is compared with Sita, ruling the three worlds cannot be equal to one-sixteenth part of Sita."
*(Sundara kanda, sarga 16, sloka 14)*

69) When Ravana was trying to seduce Sita, She is comparing herself with Other Pativratas (Wife devoted to Husbands) – "Did Suvarchala Devi, leave the Sun even though many dangers befell her? Did Sachi Devi left Indra? Rohini Devi stick to Moon, Arundhati followed Vasista, Lopamudra followed Agasthya, Savitri followed Satyavanta, Sukanya followed sage Chyavana, Srimati Devi followed Kapila, Damayanti followed king Nala, Madayanti followed king Sowdama, Kesini followed emperor Sagara, and Anasuya followed sage Atri. In the wake of many difficulties they did not leave the feet of their husbands".
*(Sundara kanda, sarga 19, sloka 3. Also sarga 20, sloka 2 - 5)*

70) Within the verdant confines of **Ashoka Vanam**, a garden of enchanting beauty designed for solace, **Sita's** captivity was a cruel paradox. Physically, she was in a seemingly idyllic setting; emotionally and spiritually, she

was plunged into the abyss of unremitting grief and profound loneliness. This particular facet of her imprisonment, the constant psychological torment inflicted by her Rakshasa custodians, is a compelling "untold fact" that paints a vivid picture of her suffering.

Ravana, in his cunning, did not leave Sita merely confined. He surrounded her with a retinue of fearsome **Rakshasa women maids**, whose primary task was to break her resolve and force her to accept him as her consort. These grotesque guardians, far from being mere jailors, were relentless instruments of psychological warfare. The Valmiki Ramayana names some of these terrifying figures: **Ekajata, Harijata, Trijata, Vikata, Ajamukhi, Durmukhi**, among others. Their appearance alone was often enough to strike terror, with their disfigured faces, hideous forms, and menacing demeanor.

These Rakshasa women, under Ravana's direct orders, employed every coercive tactic at their disposal. They "tried their best to convince Sita to become Ravana's consort," which was far from gentle persuasion. Their methods included:

- **Threats and Intimidation:** Vividly describing the gruesome consequences of her refusal, including disfigurement, torture, or even being eaten by them.

- **Descriptions of Ravana's Power:** Exaggerating Ravana's immense wealth, unparalleled might, and celestial luxuries that would be hers if she capitulated.
- **Grotesque Displays:** At times, their very presence and actions were designed to instill terror and break her spirit, offering a stark contrast to the divine purity of Sita.

Sita, despite being surrounded by the vibrant beauty of the Ashoka trees and fragrant flowers, remained an isolated figure, perpetually mourning Rama's absence and resolute in her unwavering devotion. This relentless psychological assault, a constant barrage of threats and temptations from these formidable female demons, highlights the profound depth of her agony. It underscores that her captivity was not just a physical restraint but a daily battle for her very soul, against an enemy determined to crush her spirit and desecrate her fidelity.

Sita in her mind had a doubt whether Rama going to rescue her – "As s I am away in a different country, has Rama given up his love for me?" Has he abandoned me thinking that he does not want a woman whom another man has abducted?... Going to Ayodhya…. is he happy with many other beautiful damsels? Does he speak outwardly loving words when I am in front of him and can't he be merciful when I am entangled in danger? Can Sri Rama, in fact, conquer Ravana ? He might be in some sort of sorrow! My husband has difficulties due to me and he has no happiness.

*(Sundara kanda, sarga 36, sloka 20 and sarga 26, sloka 18)*

71) Hanuman hidden himself behind tree and found time to talk to Sita when all Rakshasa Women went to sleep at Night.

*"Mother!* Your husband is anxiously waiting for you." – Hanuman said. Sita was shocked to see a Vanara talking couldn't believe her eyes and ears.

On seeing Hanuman, Sita thought very logically. 'I always think of Rama. That's why I may be hearing about him'".

Hanuman shows Rama's Ring to Sita taken from his navel.

*(Sundara kanda, sarga 32, sloka 11)*

72) When Hanuman begged Sita to come along with him from Lanka to Kishkindha, She expressed in disbelief – "You are a Monkey, how could you carry me on your shoulders! And it is not proper for me to come along with you. Let Sri Rama come and rescue me after killing Ravana.

Her words first sound strange to Hanuman and for her sake as she ridiculed him, Hanuman expanded his body and shown her his gigantic form.

*(Sundara kanda, sarga 37, sloka 29)*

73) Sita took out an ornament, which she had tied at the upper end of her garment and told Hanuman - "Give this *Chudamani* (diadem) to my husband. He will definitely believe that you met me. It is my bad luck that my husband has not yet rescued me although he is a valorous person.

*(Sundara kanda, sarga 39, slokas 9 to 12)*

74) Hanuman killed all 80,000 Soldiers sent by Ravana in Asokavana due to damages he caused by uprooting all trees.

Hanuman hit Jambumali (Son of Minister Prahasta) with Maddi tree. He also killed Aksha Kumara, Son of Ravana.

75) Ravana describes how strong Hanuman is. I had seen Vali earlier, a very strong man, Jambavan, Nila, Dvivida and other Vanaras. Their lustre and valour were not of this kind." Therefore, Hanuman has more strength than those men did!

*(Sundara kanda, sarga 46, slokas 9 to 12)*

76) After successfully locating Sita and delivering Lord Rama's message, **Hanuman** allowed himself to be captured, primarily to assess Ravana's strength and to understand the defenses of Lanka. Upon being brought before the demon king, Ravana, enraged by Hanuman's audacity and the destruction of his beloved Ashoka Vanam, decreed a humiliating punishment: the burning of Hanuman's tail, a traditional insult to Vanaras. This act, however, was about to unleash a catastrophic "untold fact" upon the unsuspecting city of Lanka.

By Ravana's direct order, the Rakshasa soldiers immediately set about their task. They meticulously **covered Hanuman's mighty tail with strips of cloth, then doused it thoroughly with oil, and finally, lit the fire.** As the flames began to engulf his tail, the citizens of Lanka, witnessing this spectacle, poured out of their homes. **Women, the aged, and the young people alike — everyone came out of their houses and mercilessly abused Hanuman,** reveling in what they believed was his humiliation. This collective outpouring of scorn and hatred highlighted the widespread animosity towards any perceived enemy of Ravana.

However, their triumph was short-lived. Hanuman, with his burning tail now a weapon, did not cower or flee. Instead, in a swift and furious display of retribution, **he thrashed the people round him,** turning their mockery into terror. Then, with a roar that shook the city, he **flew swiftly upward and fearlessly over the houses, like a lightning bolt streaking across the sky.**

What followed was an inferno of unimaginable scale. With his burning tail, Hanuman systematically **set aflame all the mansions** of Lanka. The majestic, beautiful houses of the Rakshasa capital were rapidly **filled up with thick smoke and began to burn fiercely with loud explosions,** as the flames devoured everything in their path. The city, once an impregnable fortress of gold and grandeur, quickly transformed into a roaring furnace, a terrifying prelude to the destruction that awaited it.

Finally, after ensuring that the message of Rama's impending wrath was delivered in a most spectacular and devastating manner, Hanuman, having completed his awe-inspiring act, **dipped his tail into the sea and cooled it down**, an act symbolizing his mastery over the very element he had wielded.

*(Sundara kanda, sarga 53, slokas 23 & 24)*

77) Sita Devi said to Hanuman, 'I will not live more than a month (already 8 Months Passed since abduction by Ravana). Tell these words while Sugriva listens and hand this Chudamani to Rama. Ask my husband to rescue me soon."

*(Sundara kanda, sarga 65, sloka 21 or 23)*

# YUDDHA KANDA

## (Battle among Vanaras and Daityas)

78) While praising Hanuman, Sri Rama was classifying servants into three categories. – "A servant is called the best servant if he accomplishes a difficult task assigned by his master. A servant is called mediocre if he accomplishes only the assigned task but does not do the work, which the master had not assigned even though he is capable of doing it, and is aware that his master will be happy if he did it. A servant is called base if he does not accomplish any task which his master assigns him even though he is capable of doing it."

*(Yuddha kanda, sarga 1, slokas 8 to 10)*

79) After he gave the gift of embrace to Hanuman, Rama sat again and *sank in sorrow*. The whole dejection of Rama was - how can we cross the sea and reach Lanka with Vanaras?

*(Yuddha kanda, sarga 1, slokas 17 to 20)*

80) It was Sugriva who gave the idea of building a Bridge to cross the Sea to reach Lanka.

*(Yuddha kanda, sarga 2, slokas 9 to 12)*

81) King Ravana in Lanka who lost in thought about the upcoming battle with Sri Rama and his Vanara warriors, sat with his ministers and commanders. Prahasta, Mahaparshva, Surya Satru, Agni Ketu, Rashmiketu, Indrajit, Dhumraksha, Nikumbha, Vajradhamstra, Virupaksha and many others were present.

Ravana said - I am consulting all of you not because of any fear or morality. Men in the world are of three types: the best, the mediocre, and the base.
 (a) It is the best idea if we think in accordance with what elders say traditionally.
 (b) It is mediocre if everybody thinks in his own way but arrives at a consensus after discussion and argument.
(c) It is base if everybody considers his own thought important and finds no use in consensus.

*(Yuddha kanda, sarga 6, slokas 13 to 15)*

82) Vibhishana defends Rama! "…..What harm did Sri Rama do to Ravana, the king of Rakshasas. As Khara himself transgressed and tried to attack him, Rama killed Khara in order to protect himself. Everybody in the world ought to protect their life in accordance with their strength?"

He requested Ravana to return back Sita to Rama to stop War.

*(Yuddha kanda, sarga 9, slokas 13 & 14)*

83) "Cows have the nature to provide wealth. Brahmins have a control of senses. Women are fickle minded. Kinsmen have a dangerous mentality", says Ravana. Ravana too has the same views as Rama has on Brahmins and women.

*(Yuddha kanda, sarga 16, sloka 19)*

84) In the Lanka assembly, Vibhishana abuses Prahasta, Indrajit and the king Ravana and preaches morals to them. By then the king had become furious and banished Vibhishana.

Vibhishana swiftly flew into the sky along with his followers in Pushpaka Vimana, stationed on the ground where the Vanara commanders stayed.

*(Yuddha kanda, sarga 17, slokas 2 to 5)*

85) Sugriva's opinion of Vibhishana! "Because he is the brother of Ravana, the sinner, we have to punish and kill this Vibhishana along with his ministers….We have to abandon this Rakshasa and should not admit him. This Vibhishana left his brother who is in danger. Such a man as this, whom will he follow at a time of danger?" says Sugriva.

What did he (Sugriva) do to his brother (Vali)? While his brother was fighting with the enemy (Dundubhi), did he not abandon his brother in danger, by placing a boulder so that he would not come out of the cave?...

*(Yuddha kanda, sarga 17, sloka 27 and sarga18, slokas 5 & 6)*

86) With an intense desire to cross bridge quickly, Rama said furiously. "Oh Samudra (Lord of Seas)! I will see that you sink to the level of nether world! All your waters will burn, evaporate and diminish. All the living creatures will lose consciousness and die. I will build a bridge with

the rain of my arrows and make the Vanaras cross the sea.

Samudra rose from the Sea and said - Rama! I should not give up my nature either willingly or due to fear! I will help you as much as I can. Then Rama said, "It is not possible to stop this divine arrow which I have already aimed. Where do you want me to throw it?" "Rama! I have a place called Drumakulya in the north. That place is famous like you. Some sinner's drinking water daily. I am not able to tolerate their touch.

Immediately, Rama threw the arrow where had Samudra asked him to throw it. Unable to bear that blow, the earth broke, crying for help. There the entire water that

the sinners drank evaporated. Since then, that place has become famous as *Marukantaram* (infertile land).
    *(Yuddha kanda, sarga 22, slokas 32 to 42)*

87) It took totally 5 days to build Bridge across sea of 800 miles. All Vanaras worked tirelessly in day time only uprooted many trees and brought big boulders from mountains and through them on ocean.

 They built a bridge of 14 *yojanas* length on the first day, 20 on the second day, 21 on the third day, 22 on the fourth day and 23 on the fifth day, with a width of 10 yojanas.
    *(Yuddha kanda, sarga 25, slokas 2 & 3)*

88) Ravana sent Spies Suka and Sarana and ordered, "Infiltrate into Vanara troops and collect all the secrets." They came in disguise. Sugriva's Army caught them and tortured them for a while. Sri Rama rescued them by saying Messengers should be treated well.

 Suka and Sarana reported to Ravana - "Four noble men (that is Rama, Lakshmana, Sugriva and Vibhishana) are: equal to the guardians of the world, warriors, well versed in archery, valorous and united. These four are so capable that they can destroy Lanka along with its fort.
    *(Yuddha kanda, sarga 25, slokas 29 to 34)*

89) Ravana made safety arrangements for Lanka. At the
East gate — Prahasta.
South gate — Mahaparshva and Mahodara.
West — Indrajit.
North — Ravana, Suka and Sarana.
Middle – Virupaksha

90) Rama also made plans to enter and attack Lanka –
Nila should attack Prahasta at East Gate;
Angada's Army at South Gate;
Hanuman will take over Indrajit;

Sugriva, Jambhavan and Vibhishana make a way to the Centre of the Troops and Sri Rama and Lakshmana will fight with Ravana.

91) Vibhishana's cautioned to Rama - These Rakshasas are akin to wicked Ravana in respect of valour, virility, lustre, courage and arrogance. At this moment, Rama! Do not feel annoyed! I am rousing your wrath. I am not trying to terrify you. You are capable of packing off even gods with your valour."
Since Rama is a great warrior, his enemy too should be a great warrior. Rama had to defeat such a great warrior. Hence, the poet depicts Ravana too as a great warrior.
*(Yuddha kanda, sarga 37, slokas 23 & 24)*

92) Battle began among following Pairs with soldiers on both sides:-
   Indrajit — with Angada.
 Sugriva — with Praghana.
 Lakshmana — with Virupaksha.
 Vibhishana — with Mitraghuna.
 Nala — with Pratapana.
 Rama — with Agniketu and Rashmiketu.
Hanuman — with Jambumali.
Nila — with Nikumbha.
Sushena — with Vidyunmali

93) During the fierce war in Lanka, the battlefield bore witness to a moment of profound despair for the Raghava brothers. **Indrajit**, Ravana's eldest son and a master of illusory warfare, unleashed his most potent weapon: the **Nagastra**, or Serpent Arrow. This wasn't merely an arrow; it was a mystical weapon that manifested as countless venomous serpents, binding its victims.

As this deadly volley struck, both **Sri Rama and Lakshmana succumbed to its power, fainting on the battlefield.** This shocking sight plunged the Vanara army into disarray. A truly "untold fact" in its emotional depth is Rama's immediate reaction upon regaining consciousness. While Rama himself woke after a while, **Lakshmana remained motionless, seemingly in a deep coma.** Believing his beloved brother to be dead or irrevocably lost, **Rama was overcome with unbearable grief.** His lamentations on the battlefield were heartbreaking, showcasing his profound love for Lakshmana and the sheer despair that gripped him at the thought of losing his inseparable companion and staunch supporter. He feared his mission to rescue Sita was now futile, and his return to Ayodhya impossible without Lakshmana by his side.

However, the divine cosmic order would not allow such a tragedy to fully unfold. Just as hope seemed lost, a majestic figure descended from the heavens: **Garuda**, the king of birds and the eternal sworn enemy of serpents.

This divine intervention, a powerful "untold fact" of salvation, brought instant relief. Upon Garuda's mere presence, the countless serpents that had manifested as arrows, binding Rama and Lakshmana, immediately coiled away and fled, unable to withstand the natural enemy of their kind. Garuda then gently revived Lakshmana from his coma, restoring him to full consciousness.

This incident, a testament to Indrajit's formidable magical prowess and the profound bond between the brothers, also highlights the timely intervention of divine forces in times of crisis. It allowed the epic struggle to continue, preventing an early and tragic end to Rama's sacred mission.

94) While seeing the state of Lakshma fainted; commander Sushena had an idea. He said - "In the past when battles took place between *Devas* (gods) and *Asuras* (Rakshasas) the Rakshasas who knew arms and weapons in the battle hit gods with weapons. When gods were dying in large numbers, Brihaspati chanted *Mantra Sanjivani* and healed them. Later, gods took creepers of those medicines and kept them on hills called Chandra and Drona in the sea of milk. Someone who can go quickly has to go the sea of milk and bring those medicines. It is better if Hanuman goes there."

95) The war in Lanka raged with unbridled ferocity, a clash between the righteous forces of Rama and the demonic might of Ravana. Amidst the swirling dust and the din of battle, numerous individual duels stood out, showcasing the immense valor and prowess of Rama's Vanara army. These specific encounters, often

overlooked in the grand narrative, highlight crucial "untold facts" about the direct contributions and formidable strength of various Vanara heroes as they faced Ravana's most fearsome Rakshasa warriors.

In one such fierce confrontation, the valiant **Angada**, son of Vali and crown prince of Kishkindha, faced off against the formidable Rakshasa warrior **Vajradamshtra**. Their duel was merciless, a testament to Angada's inherited strength and martial skill, culminating in his decisive victory as he **killed Vajradamshtra**, thereby eliminating a significant threat to the Vanara ranks.

Meanwhile, the mighty **Hanuman**, already renowned for his strength and ingenuity, engaged in a series of crucial battles. With unparalleled power and precision, he **killed two formidable Rakshasas: Akampana and Trisiras.** Akampana was a powerful general known for his ability to shake the battlefield, while Trisiras was one of Ravana's formidable sons. Hanuman's singular victories over these potent adversaries showcased his unwavering commitment and unmatched combat abilities.

The intelligent and powerful **Nila**, the Vanara general and son of Agni, also proved his might. In a spectacular display of brute force, he **threw a gigantic mountain** with incredible strength, crushing and **killing the formidable Rakshasa Mahodara** along with his elephant, reducing both to dust. This act demonstrated Nila's immense physical power and his ability to wield natural elements as weapons.

Other Vanara chiefs also distinguished themselves in these individual combats. The powerful **Rishabha**, wielding a club with devastating effect, **killed the Rakshasa Matta**, while Gavaksha, renowned for his brute strength, **slapped the Rakshasa Unmatta with his palm**, delivering a fatal blow.

114

96) Ravana first started with his troops. After coming to the battle ground, he sent back his troops asking them, "Protect Lanka!" He entered the battle alone!
 Ravana fainted Sugriva. Both Lakshmana and Hanuman attacked on Ravana at once.

   By the time Rama (sat on back of Hanuman) started to fight; Ravana's energies exhausted. Ravana left the battlefield on that day.


97) The battle for Lanka had already seen its share of colossal warriors, but the emergence of **Kumbhakarna** onto the battlefield sent a wave of terror unlike any other. When this truly gigantic figure, a towering embodiment of destructive power, first appeared, the very sight of him caused the **entire Vanara army to recoil in fear, many fainting** from sheer dread. This overwhelming reaction to Kumbhakarna's presence is a vivid "untold fact" that underscores his legendary might and the sheer scale of the threat he represented.

Witnessing the unprecedented panic among his forces, **Lord Rama** himself was struck by the sight of this colossal being and **enquired about this tall figure**. It was then that **Vibhishana**, ever the faithful guide, provided the crucial context of his fearsome elder brother. He narrated the extraordinary tale of **Kumbhakarna**, revealing that he was indeed **Ravana's elder brother and the son of Viswavasu**.

Vibhishana explained that Kumbhakarna was a being of immense, unbridled power and insatiable appetite, renowned for his **great valor** and a monstrous hunger that had been evident **since birth**. His voracious eating habits posed such a threat to the balance of the worlds that the gods intervened. As a result, he received a potent **curse from Lord Brahma**: he was destined to befallen by an unnatural, deep sleep for **six months at a stretch**, waking only for **one single day in a year**. It was during this brief window of wakefulness that Ravana, desperate after the losses incurred in the war, had roused him, hoping to turn the tide.

This revelation by Vibhishana explained not just Kumbhakarna's terrifying stature and power, but also the reason for his sudden, dramatic appearance on the battlefield. It highlighted that his very existence was a force of nature, controlled by a divine curse, making him a unique and terrifying adversary.

Adding a nuanced layer to the events, **Mahodhara**, one of Ravana's ministers, is also mentioned as having **made a mockery of Kumbhakarna in front of Ravana**. This detail, though brief, provides an "untold fact" about the internal dynamics of Ravana's court, hinting at either jealousy or a lack of understanding of Kumbhakarna's true strength, or perhaps a desperate attempt to rouse him from his reluctance to fight for an unrighteous cause.

Kumbhakarna's entry into the war marked a significant escalation, pitting the Vanara forces against a sleeping giant awakened for a single, devastating day of battle.

98) Kumbhakarna fought with Hanuman, Nila, Sarabha, Gavaksha, Gandhamadhana, Angada, Sugriva and Lakshmana. Besides so many warriors, he also fought with

thousands of Vanaras and ate them. After so much battle had taken place and Kumbhakarna lost his ears and nose and fainted.

99) The colossal war in Lanka reached unparalleled heights of ferocity, with both Rakshasa and Vanara armies suffering immense losses. Amidst this chaos, individual duels of extraordinary might determine the ebb and flow of victory. One such intense confrontation involved **Lakshmana**, the valiant younger brother of Rama, who faced off against **Atikaya**, another formidable son of Ravana, born of Dhanyamalini. Their battle was a testament to Atikaya's power, pushing Lakshmana to his very limits before he finally prevailed.

However, the battlefield soon witnessed an even greater catastrophe, inflicted by Ravana's eldest and most cunning son, **Indrajit**, a master of illusion and magical warfare. Unleashing a volley of his most potent arrows, Indrajit launched a devastating assault that brought the Vanara army to the brink of utter annihilation. This moment, an "untold fact" in its sheer scale of destruction, highlights the desperate situation faced by Rama's forces.

Indrajit's arrows were not mere projectiles; they were imbued with dark magic, striking vital points with terrifying accuracy. The Valmiki Ramayana grimly narrates the outcome: **"With arrows that tear the vital parts, the mighty Indrajit made Mainda, Gaja, Nila, Sugriva and Angada lifeless."** This was a catastrophic blow, as not only were countless ordinary Vanaras felled—an astonishing **67 crores** (670 million) of them—but the very core of their leadership lay seemingly dead or in a profound coma. Key generals like **Nila**, brave commanders like **Mainda** and **Gaja**, and even the King **Sugriva** and the valiant prince **Angada**, were rendered inert, their lives draining away under Indrajit's magical assault. The sight of their most prominent leaders lifeless on the ground plunged the remaining Vanaras into utter despair, their spirits shattered.

Just as hope seemed lost and the war teetered on the edge of a definitive Rakshasa victory, the divine plan intervened through the unparalleled devotion and strength of **Hanuman**. Prompted by the wise counsel of Jambavan, who recognized the unique nature of their affliction, Hanuman embarked on another miraculous flight. He swiftly journeyed to the distant Gandhamadana mountain to retrieve the fabled **Mrita Sanjeevani**, the life-restoring herb.

Upon Hanuman's return with the miraculous herb, **Jambavan**, utilizing his immense knowledge of medicinal plants and ancient lore, immediately administered the potent remedy. With the **help of Mrita Sanjeevani**

**brought by Hanuman, Jambavan saved all** the fallen Vanaras, including the critical leaders, restoring them to full life and vigour.

*(Yuddha kanda, sarga 73, slokas 43 to 45)*

100) As the war in Lanka wore on, **Indrajit**, Ravana's formidable son, repeatedly proved to be a near-invincible force, largely due to his mastery of powerful mystical rites. Recognizing the gravity of this threat, **Vibhishana**, now Rama's steadfast ally, guided **Lakshmana** to a critical location – the sacred garden of **Nikumbhila**. This covert mission to thwart Indrajit's ritual, an "untold fact" of strategic brilliance, highlights the unique blend of divine knowledge and battlefield urgency.

Vibhishana, with his intimate knowledge of Rakshasa customs and Indrajit's vulnerabilities, urgently pointed out the **fire-place of sacrifice** within the garden. His instructions were precise and grim: **"Look there! Look at that Banyan tree! Indrajit will offer sacrifice, complete the oblation to fire and come back for the battle."** He explained that Indrajit's invincibility in battle stemmed from his ability to perform a powerful *yajna* (fire sacrifice) under that specific Banyan tree. If he completed the ritual, he would become unkillable. The urgency was absolute: **"We have to prevent Indrajit from going under the Banyan tree. Kill him at once."**

This direct command underscored the strategic necessity of intercepting Indrajit before he could gain supernatural powers, an essential move to turn the tide of the war.

Thus began one of the most intense and pivotal duels of the Ramayana. **Lakshmana and Indrajit** engaged in a cataclysmic battle, unleashing a barrage of divine and magical arrows upon each other. Indrajit, drawing upon his formidable arcane knowledge, continuously fired powerful astras (celestial weapons) such as the **Roudrastra** (associated with Rudra/Shiva's destructive power), the **Agneyastra** (imbued with the power of fire god Agni), and the fearsome **Asurastra** (weapons derived from dark, demonic energies).

In response, Lakshmana, protected by divine grace and armed with celestial weapons bestowed upon him or invoked through his penance, expertly **counterattacked** with equally potent astras. He deployed the **Varunastra** (from the water god Varuna), the powerful **Sowrastra** (associated with the sun god Surya), and the mighty **Maheswarastra** (a divine weapon of Lord Shiva). Each arrow hurled was a clash of cosmic forces, illuminating the night sky and shaking the very foundations of Lanka. This battle in Nikumbhila was not just a physical fight; it was a spiritual and magical duel, fought at the precise moment to prevent Indrajit from achieving unassailable power and securing victory for Ravana.

101) Lord Rama on the advice of Sage Agastya before fighting with Ravana, recited 'Aditya Hridaya' which removes all sins, diseases, menace, fears, worries and increases longevity. Chant it and worship the sun, who is almighty!"

102) The colossal war in Lanka reached its inevitable climax with the ultimate confrontation between **Lord Rama**, the embodiment of Dharma, and **Ravana**, the mighty, ten-headed Rakshasa king. Despite Ravana's

formidable boons and his vast army, his most powerful warriors, including Kumbhakarna and Indrajit, had fallen. It was amidst this devastating realization that a profound "untold fact" concerning Ravana's inner state emerged: **Ravana, even in the thick of his final, most desperate battle with Rama, realized that his defeat was near. He knew, with chilling certainty, that Rama would conquer him soon.** (Yuddha Kanda, Sarga 109, Sloka 7).

103) Vibhishana wailed for his brother Ravana's death and later coronation has been arranged by Sri Rama whom ordered Lakshmana to do the arrangements.

*(Yuddha kanda, sarga 115, slokas 17 & 18)*

104) After the War, Lord Rama told Hanuman to take Vibhishana's permission to enter Sita Devi abode and inform Ravana's death to bring her back safely to him.
*(Yuddha kanda, sarga 115, sloka 25)*

105) upon rescued Sita from clutches of Ravana after the war, in seeing Sita came down from Palanquin, Sri Rama first rejected Sita in accepting wife in front of all Vanara and Rakshasas. He doubted her chastity being with Ravana. Sita shocked and wailed on hearing her husband's words. She requested Lakshmana to arrange a Pyre, so to sacrifice herself jumping in fire unable to bear insult.
*(Yuddha kanda, the whole of sarga 118)*

106) Agnihotra (Lord of Fire) immediately came to rescue when Sita jumped into Pyre. Agnihotra said, "Rama! This is your Sita. There is no sin in her. She has not violated you *even in heart*. Meditating about you and believing that you alone are the saviour, she rejected Ravana. I am commanding you to accept this faultless person."

"If I accept Sita who was with Ravana, the world will think that I am a fool and a lustful man, will it not? In order to create confidence of the three worlds in Sita, I kept quiet while Sita was jumping into fire. Ravana cannot even imagine about Sita who is like a flame. Sita does not expect wealth in Ravana's harem. Why do I abandon Sita? I will follow your friendly advice because you are worshipped by the world." Saying so Rama thus accepted Sita.

*(Yuddha kanda, sarga 119, slokas from 22 to the end)*

107) Indra asked Rama that what boon he wants for killing Ravana, Rama said that "all dead Vanaras should regain lives. Fruits and Roots should be available forever

for eating where Monkeys live in all seasons."
Hesitatingly, Indra deva granted this wish.
   *(Yuddha kanda, sarga 123, sloka 16)*

108) Rama preached responsibility to Vibhishana - "The invincible Lanka has been conquered since these Vanaras fought without fear for their life and without turning their backs in the battle. Felicitate them by giving gems, money and ornaments. All will realise that you are merciful, charitable and famous. You will get fame!"
   *(Yuddha kanda, sarga 125, slokas 4 to 8)*

109) With Ravana vanquished and righteousness restored in Lanka, the moment arrived for **Lord Rama** to fulfill his sacred vow and return to Ayodhya after fourteen years of exile. This journey back was not merely a logistical transition but a symbolic act of unity and gratitude, marked by a truly significant "untold fact" in the guests Rama chose to accompany him.

The vehicle for this epic return was the legendary **Pushpaka Vimana**, Ravana's celestial aerial chariot, now reclaimed by Rama. This miraculous self-propelling aircraft, capable of expanding to accommodate any number of passengers, became the symbol of Rama's triumph and the restoration of Dharma.

It was **upon the request of King Sugriva**, who, with his innate wisdom and respect for his allies, suggested that those who had sacrificed so much should witness Rama's ultimate triumph. Responding to this noble sentiment, **Rama, along with Sita and Lakshmana**, extended an extraordinary invitation. He asked **Vibhishana**, the newly crowned King of Lanka; **Hanuman**, the unparalleled devotee and hero; and significantly, **some other Vanaras and even Rakshasa Ministers** who had served Vibhishana, to join him on the Pushpaka Vimana for his coronation as King of Ayodhya.

(Yuddha Kanda, Sarga 125, Slokas 19 to 26).

110) Sage Bharadwaja tells Rama that he grasped everything about Rama's forest life by his power of penance.

Sage said – "I heard about all your sufferings in the forest. Leaving from Chitrakuta and reaching Panchavati, the abduction of Sita by Ravana. You're grieving over Sita's abduction and making friends with Sugriva, killing Vali, killing Ravana in the battle."

*(Yuddha kanda, sarga 127, slokas 16 & 19)*

111) Instead of directly meeting to his brother Bharata, Sri Rama first asked Hanuman to meet Guha (Old Man) at Sringaberipura to enquire about Bharata's attitude whether he still faithful to him in giving Ayodhya Kingdom or continue to be Its King.

*(Yuddha kanda, sarga 128, slokas 22 & 23)*

112) Hanuman (in the human disguise) saw Bharata who was served by the ministers, priests and commanders who wore yellow clothes. He also saw that Bharata was ready to jump into the Pyre as Sri Rama not turned as 14 years passed till date.

Without any delay, Hanuman told about the news of Rama's arrival. Bharata was excited and ready to offer gifts to hanuman.

Bharata said - "O gentle one! Are you a god who has come out of compassion or a human being? In return for the pleasant news, I will give you a hundred thousand cows, a hundred excellent villages and sixteen golden complexion virgin girls (as wives) of good conduct, adorned with earrings decked with all kinds of jewels and who possess a shapely nose and things, moon-like faces and rich in lineage and birth."

*(Yuddha kanda, sarga 128, slokas 42 to 44)*

113) Lifting Bharata (from his feet) whom he had seen after a long time, sitting him on his thigh, Rama felt happy and embraced him. Satrughna (first) saluted Rama and Lakshmana and then saluted the feet of Sita Devi with humility.

Bharata, who knew the essence of Dharma, brought the sandals which he had carried from Chitrakuta, and kept them near the feet of Rama and said to Rama with folded hands, "O king! I am presenting to you now the kingdom, which I have protected so far. The purpose of my birth has been accomplished as I see you again as the king of Ayodhya."

Sugriva and Vibhishana shed tears on seeing Bharata speaking so reverently to his brother.

Later, Sri Rama sat Bharata on his thigh happily and went to Nandigrama in the airplane.
*(Yuddha kanda, sarga 130, slokas 53 to 58)*

114) Rama reached Nandigrama, got down from the plane and stood on the ground. Seeing that great plane, Rama said, 'Now go back to Kubera. I have given you the order!' As Rama ordered that Pushpaka plane went toward

Kubera's mansion in the north." That plane originally belonged to Kubera. Then Ravana conquered it. Later it belonged to Vibhishana. Vibhishana had given it to Rama — either for travelling or forever.

*(Yuddha kanda, sarga 130, slokas 59 & 60)*

115) Bharata was saluting Rama every now and then. "Your Excellency! I cannot carry on the burden of ruling this kingdom! You have to accept this great responsibility.

Can a calf do whatever an ox does? Can a donkey run like a horse? Can a swan fly like a crow? I am unfit to carry on politics like you, who is a politician. Just as a fruitless tree in the backyard is useless, we do not have any use for the kingdom, which you do not rule. We have to see your coronation which will give us the utmost satisfaction of our eyes.

You have to wake up daily with the auspicious musical instruments. A great man like you must enjoy all pleasures. You have to be the king as long as the earth exists. Kindly accept my request!" Bharata prayed with folded hands.

*(Yuddha kanda, sarga 131, sloka 12)*

116) Now All the 'sages' look alike — Rama, Lakshmana, Bharata, Satrughna — became princes after an auspicious bath. Rama got into a very beautifully decorated chariot.

While Satrughna held the umbrella, Lakshmana and Vibhishana were fanning him with *Vinjaamara* (white whisks) and Bharata was riding the chariots, Rama started off to Ayodhya.

Sugriva, best among Vanaras, climbed on a hill-like elephant called Satrunjayam.

Sri Rama Chandra sat on the gem-studded throne!

*(Yuddha kanda, sarga 131, slokas 29 & 31)*

117) Rama said to Lakshmana - "Virtuous man! You also rule along with me this earth that was ruled by former kings with might. Be a prince and along with me, you too carry on the burden of this kingdom, which our forefathers ruled."

When Lakshmana did not give his consent even though being repeatedly entreated. Rama then consecrated Bharata as the prince.

*(Yuddha kanda, sarga 131, slokas 86 to 88)*

118) Thereafter, Lord Sri Rama Chandra generously gave donations to Brahmins. He gave fitting gifts to important Vanaras like Sugriva and Angada.

Sita took out a necklace of pearls from her neck and paused looking at her husband with hesitation. Rama understood and gave her permission with a smile. "Give it to the person whom you like." Feeling happy, Sita gave that necklace to Hanuman.

After his coronation, Rama ruled the kingdom and performed hundreds of sacrifices. People under 'Rama's rule' were very happy.

*(Yuddha kanda, sarga 131, from sloka 89 to the end)*

# UTTARA KANDA

## (Unfinished Chapter)

119) The **Uttara Kanda** of the Valmiki Ramayana often serves as a repository of cosmic history and ancestral tales, narrated to **Lord Rama** after his glorious coronation. One such profound "untold fact" is revealed by the venerable **Sage Agastya**, who recounts to Rama the very genesis of the Rakshasa race and their ancient dominion over the illustrious city of Lanka. This narrative provides crucial context to Ravana's lineage and the historical roots of his kingdom.

Agastya began by detailing the very first moments of life's sustenance: **"First Brahma created water."** To protect this primordial creation, he then brought forth certain living beings. These beings, faced with the stark reality of survival, were presented with a choice, their responses defining their very essence and future lineage:

- Some, driven by hunger and a primal instinct, proclaimed, **"'bhakshaamaha' (We will eat!)"** – implying a desire to consume even the water. These became the **Yakshas**, guardians of treasures, sometimes benevolent, sometimes fearsome.
- Others, choosing a path of responsibility and protection, declared, **"'rakshaamaha' (We will

**protect!)"** – signifying their vow to safeguard the water. These became the **Rakshasas**, beings destined initially as protectors, though many would later stray from this original dharma.

From among these early Rakshasas, two brothers emerged: **Heti and Praheti**. Praheti, choosing a path of righteousness and austerity, withdrew from worldly affairs to engage in severe penance. Heti, however, followed a different, less virtuous path. He married a woman named **Bhaya (Fear)**, and they bore a powerful son named **Vidyutkesa**.

The lineage continued with Vidyutkesa marrying **Salakantaka**, and their union produced **Sukesa**. Sukesa, in turn, married **Devavati**, and from them sprang three extraordinarily powerful and ambitious brothers: **Malyavan, Sumali, and Mali.** These three, driven by a desire for a magnificent and impregnable capital, approached the divine architect, **Viswakarma**, seeking his expertise to construct a splendid city. Viswakarma, with his cosmic knowledge, simply instructed them, **"Lanka is ready on Trikuta mountain. Go there!"** This pivotal "untold fact" reveals that Lanka was not a new construction but an already existing, divinely established city on the three-peaked Trikuta mountain, merely waiting for powerful occupants.

Having settled in Lanka, the three brothers established their powerful Rakshasa dynasties:

- **Malyavan** married **Sundari**, and their progeny included valiant warriors like **Vajramushti** and **Virupaksha**, among other sons.
- **Sumali** took **Ketumati** as his wife, and their numerous sons included renowned figures like **Prahasta, Akampana, and Dhumraksha** (who would later become key generals in Ravana's army). Crucially, they also had three daughters: **Pushpotkata, Kaikasi (who would become the**

> **mother of Ravana, Kumbhakarna, and Vibhishana), and Kumbhinasi.**

- **Mali** and his wife **Vasudha** also contributed to the burgeoning Rakshasa population of Lanka.

As these Rakshasas consolidated their power in Lanka, their inherent nature, combined with their growing might, began to deviate from their original protective dharma. **"All these Rakshasas settled in Lanka and began to harass sages and gods,"** turning from protectors to tormentors. This established the historical context for the perpetual conflict between the Rakshasas and the divine order, culminating centuries later in the epic struggle between Rama and Ravana.

*(Uttara kanda, sarga 4, slokas 13 & 14)*

120) Sri Rama daily morning wake starts with eulogize of Sycophants – "O king! Hero of the heroes! Lion among men! It is dawning, wake up! You are a Vishnumurti in valour. You are a Brihaspati in intellect. Mother Earth (*Bhuudeevi*) in forbearance. A Sun in lustre. Wind in terms of speed. Samudra (sea) in serenity. Moon in delicacy. No king has been born so far on the earth who is as virtuous as you are and who wished the welfare of the people. Best among men! Fame and Lakshmi (goddess of wealth) cannot leave you..."

*(Uttara kanda, sarga 42)*

121) Rama asked the spies as follows: "My citizens and villagers — What do they talk about me? What do they speak about Sita? What do they think of Bharata? What do they say about Lakshmana and Satrughna? What do they utter about my mother Kaika? They talk about the new government and the king, don't they?"

In response to this the spies said, "All the people are full of praise for your victory — that you killed the ten-headed fellow. (*dasagriva*, that is Ravana).

Again Rama asked, "Report to me in detail without leaving anything out — The good and the bad the citizens talk about…. I will hear all that and do good things. I will give up bad things. Also, inform me what the sinners in the villages say."

*(Uttara kanda, sarga 53, sloka 5 to 11)*

122) "people all over the City and Village accuse me…. As long as the words of infamy circulate, one *falls into hell.* All great people try to attain fame. Fearing slander, I will give up either my life or you. Then, where is the doubt about leaving Sita? On the other side of the bank of the Ganga, near river Tamasa, there is Valmiki's hermitage. Leave Sita over there at a spot where there are no people….. Do not speak to me about it again. Go! Do not

argue. If any one of you opposes my decision, it will cause extreme hatred for you….. If you obstruct my wish, you will be hostile to me", thus Rama spoke harshly at Lakshmana.

*(Uttara kanda, sarga 55, slokas 13 to 25)*

123) Sita Devi in tears said: "Lakshmana! Did Brahma give me this birth for the sake of lament? I do not know what sort of a sin I had committed in the past birth!

I followed the footsteps of Rama and lived in the forests. Now whom can I confide my grief? What reply should I give if the sages ask me, 'what wrong did you do, why did Rama leave you?' I will right now jump into the Ganga and give up my life".

Grieving thus for some time, finally Sita said, "Lakshmana!

Follow the orders of the king. Leave me and go. Convey my regards to all and inform them about my safety. Tell my husband as my words: 'I have a lot of respect for you. I will serve you always. You have abandoned me out of fear for disrepute. I am also obliged to remove that disrepute that you have got due to malice in the world…. For me, my husband alone is god.

*(Uttara kanda, sarga 55, slokas 3 to 17)*

124) Taking Sita to the wives of the ascetics, Valmiki said, "This is Sita. She is the wife of a good King Rama. She is Pregnant. You have to treat her with extreme care and with a sense of respect."
Consoling Sita Devi repeatedly, sage Valmiki returned to his hermitage.

Lakshmana crossed the Ganga and went back. He boarded the chariot after seeing from the other bank of the river that Valmiki had come and taken Sita with him.

While Lakshmana was feeling sad, Sumantra who was driving the chariot consoled him the following: 'In the past, Asuras who were defeated at the hands of gods, sought refuge in the wife of sage Bhrugu. Vishnu came to know that she gave them assurance and so he slayed her. Then sage Bhrugu cursed Vishnu, "You will be born in the human world. You will be separated from your wife." Hence, Vishnu was born as Rama. He got separation from his wife due to that curse. I heard this when sage Durvasa told Dasaratha this story in the past. I am telling you this secret after such a long time. Do not worry. Whatever had to happen has happened."
(Uttara kanda, sarga 59, slokas 21 to 24)

125) While the grand narrative of the Ramayana often focuses on the exploits of Rama, Lakshmana, and

Hanuman, the **Uttara Kanda** meticulously records the significant contributions of others, including **Shatrughna**, the youngest of Rama's brothers. One such pivotal "untold fact" in his saga is his heroic confrontation with the formidable Rakshasa, **Lavanasura**, and his subsequent establishment of a new kingdom.

After Rama's glorious coronation in Ayodhya, the realm began to experience peace, but not entirely. Reports reached Rama of a monstrous Rakshasa, **Lavanasura**, terrorizing the ancient region of Madhuvana. Lavanasura was no ordinary demon; he was born of **Kumbhinasi** (Ravana's sister and a daughter of Sumali) and the powerful Rakshasa **Madhu**, inheriting immense strength and possessing an unassailable divine trident given to his father by Lord Shiva. This powerful weapon rendered him virtually invincible, and his tyranny spread fear far and wide.

It was **upon receiving orders from Sri Rama** that Shatrughna, eager to contribute to the consolidation of Dharma beyond Ayodhya, embarked on this perilous mission. Rama entrusted him with a formidable task: to eliminate the tyrannical Rakshasa and establish a righteous kingdom in the afflicted region. Recognizing Shatrughna's courage and capability, Rama also bestowed upon him a powerful divine arrow to counter Lavanasura's potent trident.

142

Shatrughna journeyed to Madhuvana, confronted Lavanasura, and engaged him in a fierce and prolonged battle. Utilizing the divine arrow provided by Rama at the opportune moment, Shatrughna successfully countered Lavanasura's trident and, with a final, decisive blow, **killed the mighty Rakshasa Lavanasura.**

This victory was not merely an act of slaying a demon; it was an act of creation. After vanquishing Lavanasura, Shatrughna did not immediately return to Ayodhya. Instead, following Rama's instructions, he established a new city on the very site where Lavanasura had terrorized the populace, naming it **Madhupura** (later historically identified with the sacred city of **Mathura**). Shatrughna then embarked on a period of dedicated and just governance, **ruling his new kingdom for a period of 12 years**. During this time, he brought peace, prosperity, and righteous order to the once-troubled region, showcasing his profound abilities as a king and administrator.

His return to Ayodhya was specifically timed and for a grand occasion: **to attend the Ashwamedha Yajna (Horse Sacrifice) being performed by Sri Ramachandra**. This journey back underscored his loyalty and his participation in the culmination of Rama's reign, solidifying his unique contribution to the larger narrative of Dharma's triumph.

*(Uttara kanda, sargas 78 & 79)*

126) In the contemplative tranquility of the **Uttara Kanda**, after his glorious coronation, **Lord Rama** often engaged in deep philosophical discussions with his brother **Lakshmana**. During one such discourse, seeking to illustrate the profound efficacy and immense power of certain Vedic sacrifices, Rama recounted the extraordinary tale of King Ila, a narrative that holds compelling "untold facts" about identity, divine intervention, and the transformative power of a grand yajna.

Rama began by introducing **King Ila**, a virtuous and mighty monarch. One day, while engaged in a vigorous hunting expedition, Ila inadvertently entered a sacred grove. This particular grove held a unique and powerful curse: it was the hallowed sanctuary of **Lord Shiva and Parvati**, where Shiva himself had, in a moment of intimate seclusion, assumed the guise of a woman to enjoy the exclusive company of his consort. Shiva had decreed that any male who entered this sacred space would instantly transform into a female. Unaware of this divine edict, King Ila and his hunting party entered, and immediately, **he and all his male companions were changed into women.**

Distraught by this sudden and inexplicable transformation, Ila, now a woman, appealed to **Goddess Parvati** for mercy. Parvati, touched by Ila's plight, offered a unique and conditional boon. She pronounced: **"Be like a woman for one month and be like a man for another month."** Thus, Ila was doomed to a cyclical existence, alternating genders every month.

It was during one of her female months that Ila, in her feminine form, reached a serene lake. There, she was seen by **Sage Budha (the deity of the planet Mercury and son of the Moon-God)**. Budha was captivated by her beauty and, overcome with desire, **spent one whole month with her**. Remarkably, during this period of their union, Ila conceived. The following month, as per Parvati's boon, **Ila turned back into a male**. Despite this transformation, the pregnancy continued, and in due course, after nine months, **Ila, now in his male form, gave birth to a child named Pururavas**. This unique birth made Pururavas the progenitor of the Lunar Dynasty, an extraordinary origin story.

While Pururavas' birth brought joy, Ila's alternating gender remained a source of hardship. Recognizing his unique dilemma and the need for a permanent resolution, the great sages of the time advised him to perform a powerful ritual. They suggested the **Ashwamedha sacrifice**, a grand horse sacrifice known for its ability to fulfill even the most extraordinary desires and rectify cosmic imbalances. Through the meticulous performance of this mighty yajna, Ila finally found release from Parvati's conditional boon and **remained a male forever**.

It was this very story, demonstrating the immense spiritual power and efficacy of the Ashwamedha sacrifice to alter even divine decrees that inspired **Rama to perform such a miraculous sacrifice** for the well-being and prosperity of his own kingdom. Consequently, grand preparations began, with **sacrificial sheds being built on the sacred bank of the river Gomati in the auspicious Naimisha forest**, setting the stage for one of the most significant events in the post-war Ramayana, including the fabled reunion with Lava and Kusha.

127) Sita, who wore saffron garments looked at all those who had come to the assembly, folded her hands, bowed her head, and said with downward looks. 'I have not thought of any man other than Rama even in my mind. To me, who am the wife of Vishnu, let *Bhuudeevi*, the goddess of earth give me a place if I have worshipped only Rama.... If my words that I do not know any man other than

Rama are true, let Goddess Earth take me away!"
When Sita swore like that, a divine throne rose up from the crest of the earth. Goddess Earth appeared, embraced Sita and sat her on that throne. While Sita

was going into the nether world, rain of flowers fell from the sky."

In this manner, Sita went into the earth. She went away from Rama forever!

*(Uttara kanda, sarga 110, slokas 13 to 21)*

128) Rama did not marry again. "Without marrying another woman other than Sita, whenever he wanted to perform a sacrifice, he used to keep a golden statue of Sita beside him."

*(Uttara kanda, sarga 112, sloka 8)*

147

129) Yudhajit, the king of Kekaya sent a message to Rama through sage Gargya. "Gandharva country is very prosperous and wealthy. The river Sindhu flows in the middle of the country. You must conquer that country at any cost."

"Hearing this news, Rama was overwhelmed with joy, agreed to it and said to sage Gargya, 'O sage! The two sons of Bharata will live in that country…. Keeping Bharata in the forefront, Takshaka and Pushpaka will kill the sons of Gandharva and separate the two cities. Bharata will appoint his sons there and come back to me', said Rama and permitted Bharata to go along with the army and crown his sons".

*(Uttara kanda, sarga 113, slokas 10 to 13)*

130) In the peaceful aftermath of **Lord Rama's** reign, following the re-establishment of Dharma across his vast kingdom, the **Uttara Kanda** recounts a significant "untold fact" concerning the expansion of the Ikshvaku lineage and the strategic creation of new territories. This narrative highlights Rama's far-sighted leadership and his concern for the future prosperity of his dynasty and loyal family.

After the successful conquest of the **Gandharva country** by Bharata's forces, Rama turned his attention to his ever-devoted brother, **Lakshmana**. Recognizing the need to establish separate kingdoms for his growing family and to ensure their rightful place as rulers, Rama addressed Lakshmana with clear intent. He affirmed the capabilities of Lakshmana's sons, stating: **"Your sons, both Angada and Chandraketu, are well-versed in morals. They can rule the country. They are highly valorous. I will crown the two…"** This declaration was not merely a bestowal of power but an acknowledgment of their inherent virtues and martial prowess, making them fit leaders.

Rama then laid out the precise criteria for selecting their new domain: **"Select a beautiful place. That place should be comfortable for kings. It must be such that it is not an obstacle to others."** This instruction from Rama reflects his wisdom and foresight, ensuring that the new kingdoms would be prosperous, suitable for royal administration, and established without encroaching upon existing territories or causing conflict.

It was at this juncture that **Bharata**, ever astute and knowledgeable about the surrounding lands, offered a suggestion. He spoke of a specific territory, stating: **"There is a country called Karupadha. It is very beautiful… healthy."** Bharata's description underscored the land's aesthetic appeal and its suitability for habitation and governance. Hearing Bharata's words, **Rama immediately agreed to this proposal.** He then took the significant step of **occupying it first**—a symbolic act of establishing his sovereign claim and consecrating the land—before proceeding to **crown Lakshmana's sons, Angada and Chandraketu, as kings in that country.**

(Uttara kanda, sarga 115, up to 10 slokas)

131) The final chapters of the **Uttara Kanda** of the Valmiki Ramayana chronicle the poignant conclusion of Lord Rama's earthly reign, a series of events marked by sacrifice, divine orchestration, and the ultimate reunion with the celestial realm. These narratives, often considered "untold facts" for their somber yet profound nature, illuminate the final acts of devotion and the departure of an epoch.

The catalyst for these events was a fateful visit to Ayodhya by **Yama, the God of Death,** who arrived in the guise of a revered sage. Yama sought a private audience with **Sri Rama,** with a strict condition: no one was to interrupt their conversation, and anyone who did so would face the penalty of death. Rama, understanding the gravity of the meeting, agreed to this solemn pact. He then entrusted **Lakshmana**, his ever-loyal brother, with the critical duty of guarding the chambers, explicitly instructing him to impose the **death penalty if anyone dared to interfere**.

As Rama and Yama engaged in their clandestine conversation, an unexpected visitor arrived: the irritable and powerful **Sage Durvasa**. Known for his fiery temper and proneness to curses, Durvasa immediately demanded an audience with King Rama. Lakshmana, bound by Rama's strict command, politely but firmly conveyed: "The King is engaged in an important meeting. He cannot give permission to meet him at this moment." Enraged by this refusal, **Sage Durvasa threatened to unleash a devastating curse upon the entire Kingdom of Ayodhya.** Faced with the horrifying prospect of his beloved kingdom suffering due to his adherence to an oath, Lakshmana made a momentous decision. Out of fear for the impending curse, he reluctantly but obediently allowed the sage to enter Rama's private chambers, interrupting the sacred conversation.

Lakshmana, fully aware of the dire consequence of his action, did not flinch from his duty. To uphold Rama's promise to Yama and prevent the cosmic order from being disturbed, **Lakshmana voluntarily agreed to leave the Kingdom**. His departure was a profound act of self-sacrifice, accepting the death penalty he himself was tasked to enforce. He journeyed to the banks of the sacred **Sarayu River** and, embracing a yogic posture, **voluntarily ended his life by closing the nine apertures of his body**, ascending to his heavenly abode.

The news of Lakshmana's supreme sacrifice and departure to the celestial realms deeply affected Rama. Overcome with sorrow, and having completed his earthly mission, **Rama too took the solemn decision to sacrifice himself to the Sarayu River the very next day**. This final act of self-immersion and ascension marked the end of his glorious incarnation. In a chain of profound devotion, **Bharata and Shatrughna**, his devoted brothers, followed in Rama's footsteps, willingly relinquishing their earthly lives and ascending to the heavenly abode. Even **Sugriva**, the faithful Vanara king, later joined them, symbolizing the lasting bond forged by Dharma.

Before his departure, Rama performed his final earthly duties as a monarch. He crowned his valiant sons, **Lava and Kusha, as the kings of Kosala and Ayodhya** respectively, ensuring the continuation of the righteous Ikshvaku dynasty. He also imparted a unique and lasting directive to two of his greatest allies: **Hanuman and Vibhishana**, commanding them to **live forever on Earth**. Hanuman was tasked with remaining on Earth as a living embodiment of devotion and to guide righteous souls, while Vibhishana was to rule Lanka and uphold Dharma for eons.

*(Uttara kanda, sargas 116 to 123)*

# EPILOGUE

The timeless epic of the Valmiki Ramayana is not merely a recounting of divine deeds and human struggles; it is a sacred text imbued with profound spiritual power. As narrated by **Sage Valmiki** himself, the act of engaging with this Holy Scripture bestows immense **Phala Shruti** (benefits and boons) upon its devotees, a truly profound "untold fact" of its enduring legacy.

Valmiki, the very first poet (Adi Kavi) of this epic, unequivocally states the transformative power inherent in his creation:

- **Purity and Absolution:** The mere act of listening to or reciting even a fraction of the Ramayana holds immense purifying power. It is proclaimed that **a person will be freed from all sins if he reads just one** *sloka* **(verse), or even one line, or indeed, even one word** from this sacred narrative. This emphasizes the profound sanctity of the text, where even a fragmented exposure can cleanse the soul.

- **Honoring the Reciter:** The tradition also emphasizes the reverence due to those who transmit this knowledge. It is recommended that **one should donate clothes and gold to the person who recites the Ramayana,** acknowledging their role in preserving and disseminating this divine wisdom. This act of giving is itself considered virtuous and contributes to the blessings received.

- **Fulfillment of Desires:** Beyond spiritual purification, the Ramayana is a granter of material and familial boons. Specifically, it is stated that **by listening to the narrative of Sri Rama's coronation**—a moment of ultimate triumph and righteousness—**those who desire money will get money, and those who expect sons will get sons.** This highlights the holistic benefits, extending from spiritual liberation to worldly prosperity and familial happiness.

The overarching promise of the Phala Shruti is that **all your wishes will be fulfilled by reciting the Ramayana.** This serves as a concluding benediction, assuring devotees that their sincere engagement with the epic will lead to the realization of their deepest aspirations, both material and spiritual. It reinforces the Ramayana not just as a story, but as a living mantra capable of transforming lives.

## Types of Ramayana

To further enrich this book, readers may benefit from a concise overview of the major versions of the Ramayana across cultures and traditions. Each retelling reflects unique values, interpretations, and regional flavors, while preserving the essence of Rama's journey.

- **Valmiki Ramayana** – The original Sanskrit epic, composed by Sage Valmiki, regarded as the *Adi Kavya* (first poem).
- **Kamba Ramayanam** – A Tamil retelling by poet Kamban, celebrated for its literary beauty and devotional fervor.
- **Tulsi Ramcharitmanas** – Written in Awadhi by Tulsidas, this version emphasizes bhakti (devotion) and is widely recited in North India.
- **Adhyatma Ramayana** – A spiritualized retelling found in the *Brahmanda Purana*, focusing on Rama as the Supreme Being.
- **Ananda Ramayana** – A later Sanskrit composition, adding devotional hymns and stories not found in Valmiki's text.
- **Regional Variants** – Numerous versions exist across Asia, including the *Thai Ramakien*, *Cambodian Reamker*, and *Indonesian Kakawin Ramayana*, each adapting the epic to local culture and values.

By presenting these diverse Ramayanas, the reader is reminded that Rama's story is not confined to one text or tradition, but is a universal saga of dharma, devotion, and destiny.